The Household Inventory Guide

Ideas and Lists
for Stocking, Restocking, and
Taking Stock of Your Home

Carol Phillips

The Household Inventory Guide

Ideas and Lists for Stocking, Restocking, and Taking Stock of Your Home

Carol Phillips

Published by
IPP Press
Post Office Box 8335
Emeryville, California 94662-0335

Cover & Graphics by
Epic Design • Nevada City, California

Printed in the United States of America

Publisher's Cataloging in Publication
(Prepared by Quality Books Inc.)

Phillips, Carol.
   The household inventory guide: ideas and lists for stocking, restocking, and taking stock of your home / Carol Phillips.
   p. cm.
   Includes bibliographical references.
   Preassigned LCCN: 92-74281.
   ISBN 0-9634495-0-8

   1. Home economics–Handbooks, manuals, etc. 2. Household supplies.   I. Title.

TX326.P55 1992   640.4
                                   QBI93 -20 123

Dedicated to all those who suffered losses in the Oakland-Berkeley fire on October 20, 1991 and to the many individuals and groups who helped them start over again.

In memory of my mother
Marian Lelean Ingalls
who always said I was a good list-maker.

A Note From The Author

This book is designed to provide information in regard to the subject matter covered. The author and publisher are not engaged in rendering legal, accounting, or other professional services or advice.

Every effort has been made to make this book as complete and accurate as possible. However, there may be mistakes both typographical and in content. Although the household inventories here are very extensive, they are not 100 percent comprehensive.

Neither the author nor publisher, nor its distributors or dealers shall be liable to the purchaser or any other person or entity with respect to any liability, damage, or loss caused or alleged to be caused by this book or the information contained herein.

If you do not wish to be bound by the above, you may return this book to the publisher for a full refund.

Acknowledgments

T hanks go to the many people who helped me take this project from a dream (literally) to an actual book. Family members and friends listened, encouraged, shared ideas, checked lists, brainstormed, critiqued, and responded in ways that enabled me to complete these pages.

A large number of the people who participated in the making of this book are affiliated with the Montclair Presbyterian Church in Oakland, California. Although physically untouched by the October, 1991, firestorm in the hills around it, MPC was deeply affected by it as nearly thirty of its families were burned out of their homes. The church was very involved in helping Bay Area fire survivors start over again. Some of these fire survivors provided invaluable assistance to me throughout every phase of this book.

It is not possible to mention the names of every person who helped with the lists in *The Household Inventory Guide* because there are so many of them. But I am grateful for every idea, detail, and point of clarification offered.

Special thanks go to those who spent time reading all or part of the manuscript, giving suggestions, checking for accuracy, and providing encouragement: John Barr, Holly Chapin, Judy Cox, Cindy Crowner, Tom Debley, Linda Haswell, Louise Muhler, John Niec, Steve O'Donnell, Roland Tapp, and Bat Wallace. Thanks also to my brother, Rob Ingalls, for assistance with the business aspects of the book and to Bill Holman for his graphics work and for his patient computer coaching.

Table of Contents

1   Preface

The Household Inventory Guide is a book of ideas and lists
for setting up a household and for making inventories of
the things with which we stock our homes. The idea for the
book was conceived in the aftermath of the 1991 Oakland-
Berkeley firestorm, when over 3,000 dwellings burned to the
ground. My friends and others who lost their homes also lost
all or most of what was in their homes. Like others who have
survived upheavals, they had to start over from scratch.
Stunned and overwhelmed, they asked, "Where do I begin?"

This book is for them and for anyone stocking, restocking, or
taking stock of their homes–those who have lost their homes and/
or the contents of their homes through disaster, accident, or theft;
young people moving out of the family home or off a college
campus; newlyweds; immigrants; new owners of a second home;
couples who are separating or divorcing; and anyone wanting or
needing an inventory of personal possesions. The lists may also
be useful as a gift guide and as a basis for a wish list.

The Household Inventory Guide has two main purposes. The
first is to provide lists of common household items that serve as a
guide to stocking or restocking a home. If you are setting up
housekeeping for the first time, the lists will help you get started
and will continue to assist you as your needs grow and change.
Having lists available will diminish the guesswork if you are replacing lost household goods.

This book is also meant to act as a catalog of household items to be used for insurance, tax, or legal purposes. For instance, fire survivors not only had to figure out what they needed to begin to get their lives back together in the first days and weeks, almost immediately they had to compile lists for their insurance companies and, later, for the Internal Revenue Service. With nothing to work from this felt like an insurmountable job.

In the time that it took to complete the writing of this book, an additional use of *The Household Inventory Guide* became apparent. With fires, earthquakes, hurricanes, floods, and other disasters making frequent headlines, more and more people are feeling the need for preparedness. Being prepared includes making and maintaining current inventories of the things we keep in our homes as well as keeping a store of emergency supplies on hand. The ideas and lists in this book will help you plan if you are using them for precautionary purposes.

As a career counselor I help guide clients through a self-assessment process. Perhaps this book as an assessment tool is an extension of the work I do, which basically connects people with information. I hope that the ideas and lists in the following pages will provide the information you need for whatever purposes you are using *The Household Inventory Guide.*

2   Getting Started

How you use the lists and information in this book will depend partly on your present circumstances. You may need to read every section carefully and thoroughly. Or you may be able to skip whole sections and scan others. For everyone, though, the pages in this book are meant to be marked up and written on.

If you are new to living on your own, you will use the lists to get ideas for what you need to get started. If you are starting over because of a loss, you will be using these lists both to replace what you no longer have and to account for what you lost. Others of you will use this book as a reference for compiling your own household inventory.

If you are beginning to stock or restock your household, you will need to distinguish between what you need right now and what you may want to add later in order to live comfortably. You may need a bed to sleep in right now, for instance. If you want a headboard or canopy, you can deal with that later. You will need cutlery for food preparation but can make do without a grapefruit knife. To begin with the absolute basics, *The Short List* will get you started. The fleshing out will come in time.

If you are using the lists for insurance, tax, or legal purposes, you may be looking for specific items. After looking through page after page of these lists, one friend suggested that I call this book *It's in Here Somewhere.* While the chances are good that whatever you are trying to find *is* in here somewhere or something similar enough to remind you of it, it may not be listed exactly where you expect it to be. As you continue through the sections, however, you should be able to compile a very thorough inventory.

If you need to describe generic sounding items like refrigerator, desk, bracelets, or golf clubs, along with their prices to complete your accounting, take advantage of any available white space in this book, or use separate sheets of paper. If you are making an official-type inventory, you can translate the notes and markings you make onto whatever forms you need to fill out.

Devising a system of marking up this book will help you determine what you had or have and what you expect to get in the future. You may also need to find a way of prioritizing and of keeping track of your household items as you aquire them. You can use check marks, a numerical sytem, a color code, or whatever works best for you.

The way the lists and sections in this book are presented takes into account the various types and sizes of homes that readers have (from a studio apartment to a multibedroom house), and it also reflects the notion that how we organize our things and where we keep them is probably as unique as our fingerprints.

Keeping these differences in mind, *The Household Inventory Guide* is partly organized according to the kinds of rooms and spaces we have in our homes, such as **Kitchen, Bedroom, The Laundry Area**, and so on. These sections contain lists of things commonly found in these particular rooms or spaces except for appliances, furniture, and furnishings. Because **Appliances, Furniture & Furnishings** span all the rooms of a home, they merit a section of their own and are not usually mentioned elsewhere. That means that under **Kitchen**, for instance, you will not find stove or refrigerator. Instead, you will find dishes, a cookie jar, birthday candles, and soap—common things found on counters and in cupboards and drawers in a kitchen area. Bedding is listed under **Bedroom**, but bed is not.

Other sections list items that don't fit neatly into any one type of room or space. Examples of these categories include

Books, Pet Supplies, and equipment for Recreation, Sports & Exercise.

Some items are listed in more than one place. For example, you will find aspirin on the medicine shelf in the Kitchen, in the Bathroom, and in the "First Aid Kit" listed under Emergency Supplies. Luggage can be found both in Storage and in the Travel section.

It should be mentioned before getting to the lists that occasionally brand names are used. This should not be taken as an endorsement for any particular product. Rather, they are given as examples of a certain kind of item to clarify meaning. For instance, most of us instinctively ask for a Band-Aid when we cut ourselves, regardless of what brand of adhesive strips we use.

The Household Inventory Guide is intended for the average American person or family, and although the lists presented here probably include more than any one household would ever have, it does not include certain high-end items such as fur coats and yachting equipment. Nor does it include all the specialty gadgets like pineapple peelers, coupon clippers, and stamp holders that are easy for most of us to do without.

Because the effects of consumption on the environment is an issue constantly before us, I have included a section called Shopping Green. Shopping trends are beginning to reflect environmental concerns, both in terms of pollution control and in terms of conserving our natural resources. An ever increasing number of environmentally friendly products are on the market–everything from light bulbs to eco chic clothing to major appliances. If you are using this book as a shopping guide, this will make additional choices available to you.

3   The Short List

T his section is intended specifically for anyone starting over from scratch, having suffered a recent loss of home, including personal possessions and household goods. If this doesn't apply to you, you may skip this part and go on to the next section.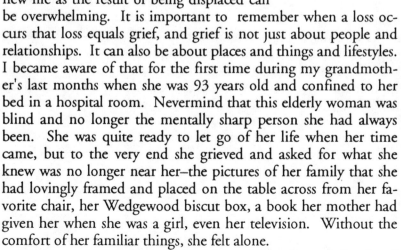

Starting over again, even under the best of circumstances, is stressful. Beginning a new life as the result of being displaced can be overwhelming. It is important to remember when a loss occurs that loss equals grief, and grief is not just about people and relationships. It can also be about places and things and lifestyles. I became aware of that for the first time during my grandmother's last months when she was 93 years old and confined to her bed in a hospital room. Nevermind that this elderly woman was blind and no longer the mentally sharp person she had always been. She was quite ready to let go of her life when her time came, but to the very end she grieved and asked for what she knew was no longer near her–the pictures of her family that she had lovingly framed and placed on the table across from her favorite chair, her Wedgewood biscuit box, a book her mother had given her when she was a girl, even her television. Without the comfort of her familiar things, she felt alone.

This lesson of grief over material loss I later learned first-hand during my divorce and again when my house was burglarized and all my jewelry stolen, including the pearls my mother had given me for high school graduation and two charm bracelets that had been years in the making.

Our homes and what we keep in them say a lot about ourselves. They become part of our identity, especially as the years pile up along side the things we accumulate. When we lose our things, we feel like a piece of ourselves is missing, and we can lose our balance. It's hard to think straight, and emotions sometimes erupt unexpectedly.

As you begin to restock your new home and itemize your losses, you will notice that many of your things can't be replaced. Because there were meanings and memories attached to those things, you will miss them and grieve. *The Household Inventory Guide* can't take the sting our of your loss, but it can help you sort through the past and point you to the future as you begin to rebuild your new life.

It may take a long time before you are able to shop for anything that is not essential. For a while thinking may be secondary to acting or reacting. Still, when you are left with little or nothing with which to begin again, you need to make quick decisions about what you need first or most in order to get on with the business of living.

This section is not a list, per se. Rather, it is meant to help you fashion your own short list according to your individual circumstances. It will act as a guide, taking you through various sections and suggesting certain items or categories of things for you to consider. Page numbers are given for each section mentioned for easy referencing.

You may expect the process of making lists to be frustrating, especially at a time when it is difficult to concentrate and focus on all that you need to do. Because the lists in *The Household Inventory Guide* are fairly comprehensive, they will appear to be cumbersome at first. Perhaps, however, you can take some comfort in the notion that the only thing worse than having to wade through so many lists, is having no lists at all.

As you read this section, it will be helpful if you use a book mark or a paper clip to hold your place as you skip back and forth between these pages and the other sections.

We begin with writing materials (i.e. paper or notebooks, pens, pencils, highlighters, etc.) so that you can start writing lists and making notes–both in this book and separately, prioritizing as you go.

If you have not done so already, pick up any prescription drugs, other medication, or first aid supplies that you use on a regular basis or expect to need immediately. You will find ideas for these in the **Bathroom** section (pages 33-35) and also in the "First Aid Kit" listed under **Emergency Supplies** (pages 48-50).

Money needs to be a top consideration. Assuming for our purposes here that you have some, the question is, how do you access it? Do you have names and numbers of your bank accounts? Do you have an adequate supply of checks? What about credit cards? Do you qualify for emergency assistance? Do you have family, friends, or a group that can provide you with what you need to tide you over?

If you have survived an area-wide disaster, it is possible that you won't need money in order to replace some of your things–at least temporarily. After the Oakland-Berkeley fire, churches, synagogues, and other groups became magnets for donations from individuals, nonprofit organizations, and corporations. Fire survivors were able to pick up such things as clothes, bedding and towels, household items, toys, and books at no cost. These same groups, as well as other organizations (i.e. Red Cross), may also be helpful to individuals who have suffered losses not associated with a local emergency.

When you have lost most or all of your belongings, you need clothes, shoes, and personal items to begin with, so turn first to the **Bedroom** section (pages 29-32) where the clothes are kept and look through the appropriate clothing lists. For now think short term. What kind of shoes, clothes, and accessories will you need in the next few days and weeks? Prioritize. Pick out what you must have, taking into account the weather and the kind of clothes you need for work or school, after work, weekends, etc.

Think in terms of what you would pack in a suitcase if you were going on a trip. My dad always used to say, "Start with your feet, and work your way up and out, so you won't forget anything."

Since you are in the **Bedroom**, you might as well scan the beginning of the list, though we'll come back for bedding later. You might want to add clothes hangers to your list and a clock, radio, or clock-radio. Jewelry is not a priority, but if you are without a watch, you may want to replace it now. Even though luggage is on a different list, you should note that you will need suitcases, boxes, bags, or something to put your belongings in. And remember that family, friends, and others will probably be more than happy to provide you with some of these basics.

Continuing to work with the mindset of packing for a trip, go now to the **Bathroom** section (pages 33-35) to pick out the personal items you need right away. Think about what you need for just one night away, and begin with the very basics like toothbrush and toothpaste, a comb, shampoo, razor, etc. Add to these essentials anything else that would make you feel more comfortable or prepared such as a blow dryer, Band-Aids, nail scissors, cologne, and so on.

If you have a baby or young child, I refer you to **Infants & Toddlers** (pages 51-53) or to **Kids' Stuff** (pages 54-55), which is probably where you would begin, even before getting your own clothes and personal items in order. What comes to mind first is equipment and supplies for feeding, diapering, and sleeping, but what you choose here will depend on the age of your child. The **Infants & Toddlers** section is comprehensive enough to accomodate little ones of various ages and stages. If you are replacing items from this list, you will want to resupply according to your child's current needs.

Because children's clothing is included in the clothes itemized in the **Bedroom** section, the **Kids' Stuff** primarily covers typical play things. If your young child has suffered a loss of home, he or she probably needs a few things in this category right away. Stuffed animals, books, and art supplies can be comforting to children and may help open up avenues to express feelings. A few toys or games can help keep a restless child occupied while you figure out what to do next.

School children may need to replace a backpack or lunch box and, of course, school supplies. A list of the latter can be found in the **Office & School Supplies** section (pages 38-40).

Similarly, if you have pets, you will want to pick up a few things for them immediately. For a list of ideas to get started, look under **Pet Supplies** (pages 56-57).

Many people who are displaced from their homes look for temporary housing while they decide on a more permanent residence. If you are relocating to a furnished home, you will probably have most of your major appliances and furniture provided for you. Still, there are a number of items that are not typically included. For instance, in the **Appliances, Furniture & Furnishings** section (pages 13-16) under "Appliances" notice which items you might need immediately, such as telephone, lamps, clock, and radio. Additional appliances are mentioned in other sections, notably the **Kitchen.**

If you are moving to an unfurnished home, you will need to spend more time reviewing the items listed under "Appliances" and "Furniture." You may also have to decide whether to rent, borrow, or buy used or new furniture, considering how best to meet both your present and future needs. At any rate, to begin with, you will need furniture to accomodate sleeping, sitting, eating, and storing your things in.

Most of the "Furnishings" listed will be low priority items for now, except for such practical things as waste baskets and garbage pail, smoke detector, and maybe a mirror. If you are without window or floor coverings, you may want to note them, too.

To begin stocking your household, it will be helpful to think in terms of what you think you will use most on an everyday basis for the next couple of weeks. Be selective at first so that your shopping time is well spent, assuming that it's not unlimited.

Let's start with the **Kitchen** (pages 17-24). You will probably need more items from this list than any other in the beginning. Even so, start with what is absolutely necessary, knowing that you will make many repeat trips to stores as you continue to restock. Let one thing double for another at the outset. A pan can do the job of a tea kettle, for example; a mixing bowl can act as a salad or serving bowl; and a paper towel can be used as a coffee filter.

Begin by choosing whatever dishes, silverware, and glasses you will need, and continue down the list. You will need some cutlery and maybe a cutting board, and assorted cooking utensils. Pick out what you think you will use most for cooking, serving, and storing food. Most of the "Electrical Appliances" you can probably do without for now, except perhaps a toaster or coffee maker.

The subsections, "Near the Sink," "Linens," and "Paper Products" have a number of items that you may use on a regular basis, but you can be more selective again when you come to "Common Herbs, Spices & Seasonings." Salt, pepper, and sugar (or their substitutes) are pretty standard in most households. While you're in the spice aisle, however, you might as well round out with a few of your favorites.

"Cooking & Basic Ingredients & Condiments," "Common Canned & Packaged Cupboard Items," and "Beverages" are subsections loaded with staples. Add to these lists whatever specific "Perishable Goods" you will need as soon as you begin to prepare meals in your home.

The subsection called "The Medicine Shelf" is placed in the **Kitchen**, but other related items are in the **Bathroom** or in the "First Aid Kit" listed in the **Emergency Supplies** section.

Next, peruse the sub-sections "Miscellaneous" and "The Junk Drawer," especially the latter to pick out those things (like scissors, Scotch tape, paper clips, and rubber bands) that we tend to take for granted until we can't find them.

Since many of us have phones in our kitchens, I'll mention address books and directories here along with a calendar and/or appointment book, borrowed from the **Office & School Supplies** list (pages 38-40).

Some linens were mentioned in the **Kitchen** section. Now add to those dishtowels, potholders, and so on whatever bedding and towels you will need. The list of bedding is given in the **Bedroom** section (pages 29-32). Although listed elsewhere, you might also include sleeping bags here if you need them. Return next to the **Bathroom** (pages 33-35) for towels and washcloths. Also, jot down toilet paper.

While in the **Bathroom**, look toward the end of the list for cleaning supplies, and note what you need. More "Cleaning Equipment & Products" are listed in the next section, **The Laundry Area** (pages 36-37) where you will find what you need for cleaning and caring for clothes and also for your home and furniture. Again, at first just choose the equipment and products you expect to use within the first week or two. If you need them now, supplies for "Outdoor Garden & Maintenance" are listed at the end of the **Oudoor Living & Maintenance** section (pages 41-43).

The **Storage** section has an assortment of items that probably deserve a good scanning. Go now to **Storage** (pages 44-47). You might want to pick up some needles and thread, for instance, and a few tools (i.e. hammer, screwdrivers, and measuring tape). You will probably need light bulbs right away and maybe batteries, string or rope, glue, and an extension cord. Depending on the weather, you might add umbrellas. Also, what about candles, flashlights, shelf-lining material, and maps. Other practical items include clothing hooks, nightlights (and bulbs), and cloth or mesh shopping bags.

You have just completed a guided tour through various sections and subsections of *The Household Inventory Guide.* I believe we have covered the high priority items and categories for most people. However, you will do well to scan the sections we skipped if they are important to you. For example, I would be hard pressed to be without at least a book or two for very long. If you are starting over from scratch, you will be adding list upon list. This section is intended merely as a place to begin.

Like the phoenix, the mythological bird that consumed itself in fire then rose from the ashes to start another long life, human beings are amazingly resilient creatures, capable of rebuilding from the remains of changed lives. Unlike the phoenix, who was a lone bird, people get help and helpers when they start over. *The Household Inventory Guide* can be one such source of help by freeing up your time to work on your most important tasks.

4 Appliances, Furniture & Furnishings

A ppliances, Furniture & Furnishings is a logical place to begin a book of lists on household goods because most of the big-ticket items in a home are in this category. Knowing what they are in the beginning will help with an overview of both the placement of these items in your home and the budgeting you may need to do when considering them. If you have to report losses of these things, the lists here will help jog your memory, although you will have to to provide the specifics.

Also, the inventories provided in the following sections on rooms are oriented more to fleshing out each room or space. These areas will appear bare without the items on this list. The **Bedroom** section lists no bed, for instance, **Dining Room** no table, **Living and/or Family Room** no sofa.

Although I have lamps, clocks, and wastebaskets in nearly all of the rooms in my home, I do not list any of these things in the room sections here. You can choose what you need from this list as you consider the various spaces in your home and add them to the appropriate lists according to your own needs.

You will notice that most of the furniture is listed as singular items. You may need more than one bookcase or sofa or desk. I am simply supplying the names of furniture commonly found in homes, while you will want to specify the number of pieces that you need. Also, some names of certain items may be interchangeable, such as bureau, dresser, and chest or coffee/cocktail table.

The list of appliances here includes both major appliances and some of the smaller ones as well. Others are listed throughout the various sections. Toaster is in the **Kitchen**, for example, and blow dryer in the **Bathroom**. "The Entertainment Center" in the **Living and/or Family Room** gives more detailed information on the television, VCR, and stereo system. The same is true for computer in the **Office** section.

Appliances

- ☐ Refrigerator
- ☐ Freezer
- ☐ Oven & Range
- ☐ Microwave Oven
- ☐ Dishwasher
- ☐ Disposal
- ☐ Washer
- ☐ Dryer
- ☐ Television
- ☐ VCR
- ☐ Stereo System and/or CD Player & Speakers
- ☐ Telephones
- ☐ Answering Machine
- ☐ Computer System
- ☐ Word Processor
- ☐ Lamps & Lighting Fixtures
- ☐ Clocks
- ☐ Radios
- ☐ Clock Radios
- ☐ Air Conditioner (Window)
- ☐ Ceiling Fan
- ☐ Portable Fan
- ☐ Portable Heater
- ☐ Alarm System

Furniture

- ☐ Bed (Frame, Box Springs, & Mattress)
- ☐ Headboard and/or Footboard
- ☐ Rollaway Bed
- ☐ Futon
- ☐ Sofabed
- ☐ Sofa
- ☐ Sectional
- ☐ Loveseat
- ☐ Bench

Chairs

- ☐ Dining room
- ☐ Kitchen
- ☐ Bar Stools
- ☐ Leisure
- ☐ Lounge
- ☐ Parlor
- ☐ Wing

- ☐ Desk
- ☐ Office
- ☐ Folding
- ☐ Beanbag
- ☐ Stepladder
- ☐ Rocker
- ☐ Recliner
- ☐ Director's
- ☐ Vanity Stool
- ☐ Ottoman
- ☐ Hassock

Tables

- ☐ Dining
- ☐ Kitchen
- ☐ Coffee/Cocktail
- ☐ End
- ☐ Occasional
- ☐ Lamp
- ☐ Bedside
- ☐ Sofa
- ☐ Parson's
- ☐ Plant
- ☐ Mail
- ☐ Sofa Back
- ☐ Folding
- ☐ TV Tray Tables
- ☐ Card
- ☐ Drafting
- ☐ TV Stand
- ☐ Butcher's Block
- ☐ Tea Cart
- ☐ Work Bench
- ☐ Desk
- ☐ Bureau
- ☐ Dresser
- ☐ Chest

- ☐ Cabinet
- ☐ China Cabinet
- ☐ Buffet
- ☐ Hutch
- ☐ Breakfront
- ☐ Armoir
- ☐ Wardrobe
- ☐ Storage Trunk
- ☐ Hope Chest
- ☐ Large Musical Instruments (i.e.Piano, Organ, Drum Set)
- ☐ Bookcase
- ☐ Wall Unit
- ☐ Shelf Unit
- ☐ File Cabinet
- ☐ Office/Computer Group (i.e. Desk, Hutch, Printer Stand, Corner Connector)
- ☐ Sewing Machine with Cabinet

Furnishings

Floor Coverings

- ☐ Carpets
- ☐ Rugs
- ☐ Pads

Window Coverings

- ☐ Draperies
- ☐ Curtains
- ☐ Shades
- ☐ Blinds
- ☐ Shutters
- ☐ Valences

Things That Hang on Walls

- ☐ Fine Art
- ☐ Mirrors
- ☐ Tapestry
- ☐ Wallhangings

- [ ] Paintings
- [ ] Framed Pictures, Photographs, Handwork, Diplomas, etc.
- [ ] Plates & Platters with Hanging Plate Holders
- [ ] Posters
- [ ] Plaques
- [ ] Shadow Box with Collections
- [ ] Display Racks
- [ ] Barometer
- [ ] Sconces
- [ ] Clocks
- [ ] Lighting Fixtures
- [ ] Wreath
- [ ] Bulletin Board & Push Pins
- [ ] Chalk Board & Chalk
- [ ] Halltree/Coat Rack
- [ ] Umbrella Stand
- [ ] Chandelier
- [ ] Chimes
- [ ] Decorator Pillows
- [ ] Book Ends
- [ ] Antiques & Collectibles
- [ ] Sculpture
- [ ] Figurines
- [ ] Statues
- [ ] Music Box
- [ ] Framed Photographs
- [ ] Plates and Platters
- [ ] Plate Display Stands
- [ ] Planters

- [ ] Plants (Live and/or Artificial)
- [ ] Vases
- [ ] Baskets
- [ ] Bowls
- [ ] Pots
- [ ] Boxes
- [ ] Candlesticks
- [ ] Oil Lamp
- [ ] Decanters
- [ ] Ash Trays
- [ ] Doilies
- [ ] Artificial Fruit
- [ ] Paper Weight
- [ ] World Globe
- [ ] Wastepaper Baskets
- [ ] Garbage Pail
- [ ] Recycling Receptacles
- [ ] Fire Extinguisher (A-B-C Rating, Halon-free)
- [ ] Stepping Stool
- [ ] Ladder
- [ ] Holiday & Seasonal Decorations (i.e. Christmas Tree Stand, Skirt, Lights, & Tree & Table Ornaments; Menorah, Dradle; Decorations for Fourth of July, Halloween , Thanksgiving, etc.)
- [ ] Religious Items (i.e. Cross, Crucifix ,Seder Plate, Scrolls)
- [ ] Smoke Detectors
- [ ] Protector Pads (Felt or Cork)
- [ ] Potpourri & Accessories (i.e. Decorative, Simmering, Crystals, Oil, Pot)

5 Kitchen

W hen asked what their favorite room is, many people think of the kitchen. It is often considered the heart of our homes because it is the source of our nourishment and a place where we cook and eat and laugh together.

The lists here are fairly self-explanatory except that the location of some of the items are arbitrarily placed in a particular category when they could be placed in another subsection just as well. Dish cloths and dish towels, for instance, are listed under "Linens" instead of "Near the Sink," although they belong in both places. Coffee filters are in the subsection "Cooking & Storage Equipment & Aids" rather than on the "Paper Products" list because some filters are made of cloth, not paper.

Most of us have what I call "The Junk Drawer," a catch-all space where we keep small, miscellaneous things handy. It may be a shoe box in a cupboard instead, and it may be in a different room entirely. But it is given here because the kitchen is often a central, catch-all kind of place.

Tableware

Set of Dishes

- ☐ Dinner Plates
- ☐ Salad Plates
- ☐ Dessert Plates
- ☐ Bread & Butter Plates
- ☐ Bowls (Cereal/Soup)
- ☐ Cups & Saucers

☐ Coffee Mugs

☐ Misc. Bowls (i.e. Fruit Compotes)

☐ Covered Butter Dish

Flatware

- ☐ Place Knives
- ☐ Butter Knives
- ☐ Steak Knives
- ☐ Place Forks
- ☐ Salad Forks
- ☐ Teaspoons
- ☐ Tablespoons
- ☐ Grapefruit Spoons

☐ Divided Flatware Organizer

Glassware

- ☐ Drinking Glasses, Various Sizes
- ☐ Wine Glasses

Cooking Utensils

Cutlery

- ☐ Assorted Cutting Knives (i.e. Peeling, Paring, Vegetable, Serrated, Utility, Sandwich, Filet, Boning, Carving, Slicing, French Cook's, Cleaver, Bread)

☐ Knife Rack

☐ Knife Sharpener (Butcher's Steel or Whetstone)

☐ Cutting Board

☐ Can Opener

☐ Bottle Opener

☐ Wine Opener (i.e. Corkscrew, Cork Puller)

☐ Jar Opener

☐ Stirring Spoons

☐ Slotted Spoon

☐ Ladle

☐ Spoon Rest

☐ Spatulas, Assorted

☐ Potato Peeler

☐ Grater

☐ Cheese Slicer

☐ Rubber Scraper

☐ Whisk

☐ Tongs

☐ Two-Pronged Cook's Fork

☐ Pasta Server

☐ Measuring Spoons

☐ Measuring Cups (Nest for Dry Measure; Glass or Plastic, Assorted Sizes)

☐ Colander

☐ Strainers

☐ Steamer Inset

☐ Egg/Rotary Beater

☐ Potato Masher

☐ Funnels (1 Wide-mouthed)

☐ Garlic Press

☐ Mallet and/or Meat Pounder

☐ Chopping Bowl & Chopper

- ☐ Mortar & Pestle
- ☐ Flour Scoop
- ☐ Flour Sifter
- ☐ Cookie Cutters
- ☐ Cookie Gun
- ☐ Pastry Blender
- ☐ Rolling Pin
- ☐ Rolling Pin Cover & Cloth
- ☐ Pastry Crimper & Sealer
- ☐ Pastry Decorating Set
- ☐ Icing Spatula
- ☐ Utility Scissors
- ☐ Basting Brush
- ☐ Baster
- ☐ Skimmer
- ☐ Juicer
- ☐ Citrus Peeler
- ☐ Apple Corer
- ☐ Lemon Zester
- ☐ Grapefruit Knife
- ☐ Nutcracker & Picks
- ☐ Fish Scaler
- ☐ Pizza Wheel
- ☐ Skewers
- ☐ Poultry Lacers
- ☐ Trussing Needles
- ☐ Butcher's Twine
- ☐ Turkey Pins
- ☐ Cheesecloth
- ☐ Jigger
- ☐ Bar Shaker

Serving Pieces

- ☐ Carving Set
- ☐ Cheese Spreader
- ☐ Demitasse Spoons
- ☐ Gravy Ladle
- ☐ Ice Cream Scoop
- ☐ Large Spoons (1 Slotted)
- ☐ Cake Knife
- ☐ Pie Server
- ☐ Salad Servers
- ☐ Two-tined Fork (To reach bottom of jars)

Cooking & Storage Equipment & Aids

- ☐ Food Scale
- ☐ Timer
- ☐ Egg Timer
- ☐ Bottle Stoppers
- ☐ Hot Pads and/or Trivets
- ☐ Oven Thermometer
- ☐ Refrigerator Thermometer
- ☐ Meat Thermometer
- ☐ Candy Thermometer
- ☐ Tea Diffuser
- ☐ Coffee Filters
- ☐ Toothpicks
- ☐ Matches
- ☐ Butter Dish
- ☐ Salt & Pepper Shakers
- ☐ Pepper Mill
- ☐ Creamer & Sugar Bowl
- ☐ Pitchers, Small (Syrup, Gravy, etc.)
- ☐ Pitchers and/or Jugs, Large (Beverage)
- ☐ Thermos
- ☐ Insulated Cold Drink Containers
- ☐ Mixing Bowls (Nest)
- ☐ Bread Box/Bin

- [ ] Storage Containers, Assorted Sizes & Shapes (i.e. Flour, Sugar, Pasta, Coffee, Tea, Crackers, Cookies, Dried Fruit, Leftovers, Misc.)
- [ ] Canning Jars
- [ ] Storage Jars
- [ ] Cookie Jar
- [ ] Pie Plate Cover
- [ ] Covered Cake Plate
- [ ] Casserole Dishes, Assorted Sizes (Some Covered)
- [ ] Souffle Molds & Ramekins
- [ ] Baking Pans, Assorted Sizes & Shapes & Depths
- [ ] Cookie Sheets
- [ ] Pie Sheet
- [ ] Serving Bowls, Assorted Sizes (Some Covered)
- [ ] Salad Bowls
- [ ] Gravy Boat
- [ ] Platters
- [ ] Large Meat/Poultry Platter for Carving
- [ ] Assorted Hors 'Doeuvre Serving Pieces for Chips & Dip, Crackers & Cheese, Condiments,etc.: Plates, Trays, Bowls, Platters, Baskets
- [ ] Serving Tray (For breakfast in bed or sick tray)
- [ ] Bread Trays & Baskets
- [ ] Ice Bucket & Tongs
- [ ] Fruit Bowl or Basket
- [ ] Heat Diffuser
- [ ] Wine Rack
- [ ] Frying/ Saute Pans, Assorted Sizes (Some Covered)
- [ ] Wok or Stir-fry Pan
- [ ] Griddle
- [ ] Sauce Pans with Lids, Assorted Sizes
- [ ] Dutch Oven
- [ ] Stockpot
- [ ] Broiling Pans
- [ ] Roasting Pan & Rack
- [ ] Verticle Poultry Rack
- [ ] Double Boiler
- [ ] Pressure Cooker
- [ ] Omelet Pan
- [ ] Pizza Pan
- [ ] Loaf Pans
- [ ] Pie Plates
- [ ] Muffin Tins
- [ ] Cooling Racks
- [ ] Teakettle
- [ ] Teapot
- [ ] Microwave-safe Cookware
- [ ] Fondue Set
- [ ] Gelatin/Aspic Molds
- [ ] Candy Molds
- [ ] Spice Rack
- [ ] Recipe Box & Cards
- [ ] Recipe Card Rack
- [ ] Cook Books
- [ ] Ice Trays
- [ ] Egg Coddlers
- [ ] Lazy Susan

Electrical Appliances

- [ ] Blender
- [ ] Coffee Maker
- [ ] Crock Pot
- [ ] Food Processor
- [ ] Micro-processor

- ☐ Microwave
- ☐ Mixer (Hand-held and/or Stand)
- ☐ Skillet and/or Wok
- ☐ Toaster
- ☐ Toaster Oven
- ☐ Waffle Iron
- ☐ Can Opener

Gourmet or Specialty Items

- ☐ Coffee Grinder
- ☐ Specialty Coffee Maker (i.e. Espresso, Cappuccino)
- ☐ Pasta Maker
- ☐ Grain Mill
- ☐ Bread Machine
- ☐ Ice Crusher
- ☐ Sandwich Maker
- ☐ Popcorn Popper
- ☐ Ice Cream Maker
- ☐ Yogurt Maker
- ☐ Deep Fat Fryer with Basket
- ☐ Tiered Steamer
- ☐ Fish Poacher with Rack
- ☐ Fondue Set with Fuel
- ☐ Rice Cooker
- ☐ Pizza Stone/Brick
- ☐ Tortilla Maker
- ☐ Portable Barbecue Pit Smoker
- ☐ Food & Meat Chopper or Grinder
- ☐ Meat Slicer
- ☐ Mouli Julienne
- ☐ Citrus Juicer
- ☐ Soda Siphon
- ☐ Salad Spinner

Near the Sink

- ☐ Garbage Pail
- ☐ Soap Dish & Soap Bar
- ☐ Liquid Soap Dispenser & Liquid Soap
- ☐ Sponges
- ☐ Dishpan
- ☐ Sink Mat
- ☐ Dish Drainer/Drying Rack
- ☐ Dishwashing Detergent
- ☐ Dishwasher Detergent
- ☐ Jet Dry
- ☐ Scouring & Abrasive Nylon Pads
- ☐ Cleaning Brushes
- ☐ Vegetable Brush
- ☐ Cleanser
- ☐ Ammonia
- ☐ Silver Polish
- ☐ Sink Stopper
- ☐ Faucet Aerator
- ☐ Swivel Spray Aerator
- ☐ Hand Lotion

Linens

- ☐ Potholders & Oven Mitts
- ☐ Dish Cloths
- ☐ Dish Towels (Tea Towels & Terry Towels)
- ☐ Cloth Napkins & Napkin Rings
- ☐ Tablecloths
- ☐ Placemats
- ☐ Aprons

Paper Products

- ☐ Paper Towels
- ☐ Napkins

- ☐ Cups (Cold Beverage, Hot Beverage)
- ☐ Shelf-lining Paper
- ☐ Plates
- ☐ Lunch Bags
- ☐ Food Wrap
- ☐ Foil Wrap
- ☐ Waxed Paper
- ☐ Kitchen Parchment (Non-stick Pan-liner)
- ☐ Sandwich Bags
- ☐ Food Storage Bags
- ☐ Freezer Bags
- ☐ Baking Cups

Common Herbs, Spices & Seasonings

- ☐ Allspice
- ☐ Basil
- ☐ Bay Leaves
- ☐ Beau Monde
- ☐ Beef Bouillon Cubes
- ☐ Cayenne Pepper
- ☐ Celery Seed or Salt
- ☐ Chicken Bouillon Cubes
- ☐ Chicken Seasoned Stock Base
- ☐ Chili Powder
- ☐ Chives
- ☐ Cinnamon
- ☐ Cloves (Whole & Powdered)
- ☐ Cream of Tartar
- ☐ Cumin
- ☐ Curry Powder
- ☐ Dill
- ☐ Food Coloring
- ☐ Garlic Powder or Salt
- ☐ Ginger

- ☐ Italian Seasoning
- ☐ Maple Flavoring
- ☐ Marjoram
- ☐ Mustard Powder
- ☐ Nutmeg
- ☐ Onion Salt, Powder, or Flakes
- ☐ Oregano
- ☐ Paprika
- ☐ Parsley Flakes
- ☐ Pepper
- ☐ Peppercorns
- ☐ Poultry Seasoning
- ☐ Rosemary
- ☐ Sage
- ☐ Salt
- ☐ Salt Substitute
- ☐ Seasoning Salt
- ☐ Sugar Substitute
- ☐ Sugar, Brown
- ☐ Sugar, Granulated
- ☐ Sugar, Powdered
- ☐ Tarragon
- ☐ Thyme
- ☐ Vanilla Flavoring

Cooking & Baking Ingredients & Condiments

- ☐ Oil (i.e. Vegetable, Olive)
- ☐ Vinegar (i.e. Apple Cider, White, Red Wine)
- ☐ Soy Sauce
- ☐ Worcestershire Sauce
- ☐ Teriyaki Sauce
- ☐ Barbecue Sauce
- ☐ Taco Sauce
- ☐ Catsup
- ☐ Mustard, Various Kinds

- ☐ Mayonnaise
- ☐ Pickles (Dill, Sweet)
- ☐ Pickle Relish
- ☐ Tabasco Sauce
- ☐ Horseradish
- ☐ Tartar Sauce
- ☐ Packaged Sauces & Mixes
- ☐ Peanut Butter
- ☐ Jam/Jelly
- ☐ Honey
- ☐ Molasses
- ☐ Maple Syrup
- ☐ Flour
- ☐ Wheat Germ
- ☐ Baking Soda
- ☐ Baking Powder
- ☐ Shortening
- ☐ Cooking Spray
- ☐ Corn Syrup
- ☐ Baking/Pancake Mix
- ☐ Corn Meal
- ☐ Cocoa
- ☐ Gelatin
- ☐ Tapioca
- ☐ Salad Dressing
- ☐ Salsa
- ☐ Olives
- ☐ Pimentos
- ☐ Water Chestnuts
- ☐ Chutney
- ☐ Capers
- ☐ Nuts (i.e. Walnuts, Almonds)
- ☐ Chocolate Chips

Common Canned & Packaged Cupboard Items

- ☐ Soups
- ☐ Beans, Assorted Dry & Canned (i.e. Kidney, Baked, Refried)
- ☐ Tomato Sauce
- ☐ Tomato Paste
- ☐ Pasta Sauce
- ☐ Peeled Tomatoes
- ☐ Meat & Fish (i.e. Deviled Ham, Tuna, Shrimp, Clams)
- ☐ Vegetables
- ☐ Fruit
- ☐ Evaporated Milk
- ☐ Condensed Milk
- ☐ Powdered Milk
- ☐ Non-Dairy Creamer
- ☐ Cereal
- ☐ Hot Cereal
- ☐ Pasta
- ☐ Rice
- ☐ Snack Foods (i.e. Popcorn, Nuts, Crackers, Cookies, Raisins)

Beverages

- ☐ Juices
- ☐ Soft Drinks & Mixers
- ☐ Bottled Water
- ☐ Coffee
- ☐ Tea

    Alcoholic
    - ☐ Beer
    - ☐ Wine
    - ☐ Hard Liquor (i.e. Bourbon, Scotch, Gin, Vodka, Brandy)

Perishable Goods

- ☐ Fresh Fruit
- ☐ Fresh Vegetables
- ☐ Bread & Other Bakery Products

- [ ] Dairy Products
- [ ] Meat, Fish & Poultry
- [ ] Frozen Foods & Beverages

The Medicine Shelf

- [ ] Vitamins & Minerals
- [ ] Oral Prescription Medications
- [ ] Aspirin and/or Aspirin Substitutes
- [ ] Antacid
- [ ] Cough Medicine
- [ ] Cough Drops
- [ ] Cold and/or Allergy Medication
- [ ] Measuring Vial
- [ ] Pill Containers

Miscellaneous

- [ ] Paper Plate Holders
- [ ] Paper Towel Holder
- [ ] Bag Clips
- [ ] Space Organizers (i.e. Turntables, Stoarage Baskets, Cup Hooks, China Rack)
- [ ] Space Savers (i.e. Bi-level Turntables, Expandable Trays with Collapsible Legs)
- [ ] Refrigerator Magnets
- [ ] Empty Coffee Cans, Jars, Margarine Tubs for Extra Storage Containers
- [ ] Grease Can
- [ ] Straws
- [ ] Birthday Candles
- [ ] Toothpicks (Plain for Baking & Fancy for Hors'Doeuvres)

- [ ] Calendar
- [ ] Air Freshener
- [ ] Lunch Pail
- [ ] Cloth or Mesh Shopping Bags

The Junk Drawer

- [ ] Scissors
- [ ] Scratch Paper
- [ ] Pens
- [ ] Pencils
- [ ] Colored Marking Pens and/or Pencils
- [ ] Scotch Tape
- [ ] Masking/Freezer Tape
- [ ] Paper Clips
- [ ] Ruler
- [ ] Measuring Tape
- [ ] Rubber Bands
- [ ] Post-it Notes
- [ ] Thumb Tacks
- [ ] String
- [ ] A Few Tools (i.e. Screwdrivers, Hammer, Pliers)
- [ ] Envelopes
- [ ] Stamps
- [ ] Return Address Labels or Stamp & Pad
- [ ] Flashlight
- [ ] Matches
- [ ] Spare Keys
- [ ] Gum
- [ ] Candy
- [ ] Wine Corks

6   Dining Room

Not everyone has a formal dining room, but even those who don't have a separate room for eating meals may have some of the things listed here. Admittedly, most of these items wouldn't make it on a priority list of things that we *need* to set up a household. Nevertheless, they are nice to have for those special occasions, holiday gatherings, or for entertaining guests.

Dining Room
- [ ] Table Pads
- [ ] Table Cloths and/or Runners
- [ ] Placemats
- [ ] Napkins
- [ ] Napkin Rings
- [ ] Trivets
- [ ] Hot Pads
- [ ] Centerpiece(s)
- [ ] Candlesticks

Set of "Good" Dishes
- [ ] Dinner Plates
- [ ] Salad Plates
- [ ] Bread & Butter Plates
- [ ] Soup Bowls
- [ ] Dessert Bowls & Plates
- [ ] Cups & Saucers
- [ ] Miscellaneous and/or Demitasse Cups Plates & Saucers

Silverware
- [ ] Dinner or Place Knives
- [ ] Butter Knives
- [ ] Dinner or Place Forks

☐   Salad Forks
☐   Teaspoons
☐   Tablespoons
☐   Miscellaneous
    Serving Pieces
    (Department or
    jewelry stores with a
    bridal registry have
    very complete lists of
    these pieces.)

☐ Silverware Storage Chest

Glassware & Stemware

☐   Goblets
☐   Wine Glasses
☐   Champagne Glasses
    and/or Flutes
☐   Bar Glasses, Assorted
    Sizes & Shapes
    (Highball, Martini,
    Snifter, Cordial, etc.)

☐ Punchbowl, Cups &
  Ladle
☐ Pitcher(s)

Tea Service

☐   Tray
☐   Coffee Server
☐   Tea Server
☐   Creamer
☐   Sugar Bowl & Tongs
☐   Slop Bowl

☐ Salt & Pepper Shakers
☐ Cruet Set
☐ Food Warmer
☐ Serving Bowls (Some
  Covered)
☐ Serving Plates & Platters
☐ Well & Tree Platter
☐ Condiment Dishes & Bowls
☐ Relish Tray
☐ Bread Tray
☐ Gravy Boat & Ladle
☐ Plate Organizer
☐ Wine Cooler and/or Bottle
  Coaster

7 Living and/or Family Room

T hese rooms have been combined here because the two rooms tend to serve
a similar purpose. People use these
rooms primarily to relax, to entertain,
or to be entertained. We often associate
them with listening to music, watching
television, reading, and playing games.
Much of what is normally found in a
living room or a family room appears in the **Appliances,
Furniture & Furnishings** section where you will find things like
sofa, table, chairs, lamps, and so on. The items on this list flesh
out these rooms rather than furnish them.

Living and/or Family Room

Entertainment Center

- ☐ Television
- ☐ VCR
- ☐ Stereo System
  - ☐ AM/FM Tuner
  - ☐ Cassette Player
  - ☐ Compact Disc Player
  - ☐ Turntable
- ☐ Reel-to-Reel Tape Player
- ☐ Speakers
- ☐ Video Game Player
- ☐ Video Cassettes & Rack
- ☐ Cassette Tapes & Rack
- ☐ Compact Discs & Rack
- ☐ Records & Rack
- ☐ Video Games & Rack

- [ ] TV Stand
- [ ] Demagnetizer
- [ ] Record Cleaning Fluid & Applicator
- [ ] Cassette Tape Cleaner
- [ ] Portable Cassette Player
- [ ] Portable Tape Recorder
- [ ] Portable Radio
- [ ] Headphones
- [ ] Walkman
- [ ] Board & Other Games (i.e. Monopoly, Tripoli, Scrabble, Checkers, Chess, Dominoes, Cribbage, Aggravation, Backgammon, Dungeons & Dragons,Yahtzee, Trivial Pursuit, Pictionary, etc.)
- [ ] Game Parts (i.e. Poker Chips, Dice, Marbles)
- [ ] Instruction Book and/or Booklets on Card & Board Games
- [ ] Playing Cards

- [ ] Score Cards & Sheets
- [ ] Bridge Tallies & Score Pads
- [ ] Paper
- [ ] Pencils
- [ ] Drink Coasters
- [ ] Cocktail Napkins
- [ ] Coffee Table Book

Fireplace
- [ ] Screen
- [ ] Grate or Andirons
- [ ] Fire Tools
  - [ ] Poker
  - [ ] Tongs
  - [ ] Shovel
  - [ ] Brush
- [ ] Bellows
- [ ] Matches & Container
- [ ] Long Matches
- [ ] Wood Holder
- [ ] Magazine Rack
- [ ] Newspaper Holder

8 Bedroom

(Including Clothes)

L ike the other room lists, the bedroom list does not include the things we probably associate most with this particular room. That's because many of the items commonly found in a bedroom, like bed, dresser, lamps, and so on are listed under **Appliances, Furniture & Furnishings**.

Included here, along with bedding and some miscellaneous items typically found in the bedroom, are things we tend to keep in our closets and drawers–namely clothes and accessories.

Some of the clothes and shoes in this inventory are listed in a general way. You will probably want to make distinctions within certain categories to further define your own needs. A woman's casual shoes could mean loafers, flats, or moccasins to name just a few examples. Dresses can be casual, dressy, or formal and also vary according to the weather and seasons. Some men have quite a collection of hats and caps, reflecting not only seasonal needs, but also occupational choices or avocational interests.

Because there are more similarities than differences between adult and children's clothing, all clothes are grouped together here even though not everything will apply to the young people.

Bedroom (Including Clothes)

Bedding

- [ ] Pillows
- [ ] Mattress Pads
- [ ] Sheets (Fitted & Top)
- [ ] Pillow Cases
- [ ] Blankets
- [ ] Bedcover (i.e. Bedspread, Quilt, Comforter or Comforter Set)
- [ ] Extra Pillows & Shams
- [ ] Throw Pillows
- [ ] Reading Pillow/Back Rest

- [ ] Clock
- [ ] Radio or Clock Radio
- [ ] Closet Organizers and/or Space Savers
- [ ] Under-the-Bed Storage Unit
- [ ] Garment Bags
- [ ] Assorted Clothes Hangers (i.e. Regular, Skirt, Slacks, Suit, Coat)
- [ ] Shoe Racks and/or Hangers
- [ ] Clothes Hamper or Basket
- [ ] Tie Rack
- [ ] Belt Rack
- [ ] Extra Clothing Hooks (Screw-type or Stick-on)
- [ ] Cedar Chips or Blocks for Closets
- [ ] Dresser Organizer (for Keys, Change, etc.)
- [ ] Jewelry Box

Jewelry

- [ ] Rings
- [ ] Bracelets
- [ ] Watches
- [ ] Necklaces and/or Chains
- [ ] Pendants
- [ ] Pins/Brooches
- [ ] Earrings
- [ ] Scarf Holders
- [ ] Tie Clips
- [ ] Cufflinks

- [ ] Money Clip
- [ ] Shoe Horn
- [ ] Extra Shoe Laces
- [ ] "Keepers" (Shoulder Strap Guards)
- [ ] Safety Pins, Assorted Sizes
- [ ] Full Length Mirror

Women's and Girls' Clothes & Accessories

Shoes

- [ ] Sneakers
- [ ] Casual
- [ ] Dress
- [ ] Sandals
- [ ] Boots
- [ ] Slippers

- [ ] Nylons (Hosiery)
- [ ] Knee Highs
- [ ] Socks
- [ ] Underpants
- [ ] Control Briefs (Used to be called Girdles)
- [ ] Bras
- [ ] Camisoles
- [ ] Slips
- [ ] Teddy and/or Other Special Lingerie

☐ Thermal Underwear
☐ Tights
☐ Jeans
☐ Casual Pants
☐ Slacks
☐ Shorts
☐ Skirts
☐ Vests
☐ Suits
☐ Dresses (i.e. Casual, Daytime, Cocktail, Formal)
☐ Blouses (i.e. Long Sleeve, Short Sleeve)
☐ Shirts & Tops (i.e. Turtleneck, T-shirt, Polo)
☐ Sweaters (Cardigan & Pull-over)
☐ Blazers
☐ Sweatshirts
☐ Sweatpants
☐ Jogging/Exercise/Sports Outfits
☐ Jackets (i.e. Windbreaker, All-weather Coat, Parka)
☐ Coats (i.e. Rain, Heavy, Dress)
☐ Poncho, Shawl, Miscellaneous Wraps
☐ Uniforms
☐ Nightgowns and/or Pajamas
☐ Bathrobes
☐ Bedjacket
☐ Belts
☐ Purses
☐ Scarves and/or Ties
☐ Handkerchiefs
☐ Gloves
☐ Mittens
☐ Mufflers

☐ Hats
☐ Bathing Suits
☐ Bathing Suit Cover-up

Men's and Boys' Clothes & Accessories

Shoes
☐ Sneakers
☐ Casual
☐ Dress
☐ Thongs, Sandals, and/or Huaraches
☐ Slippers
☐ Boots

☐ Socks (Athletic & Dress)
☐ Underpants
☐ Athletic Supporters
☐ Undershirts
☐ Thermal Underwear
☐ Jeans
☐ Casual Pants
☐ Slacks
☐ Shorts
☐ Dress Shirts (i.e. Long Sleeve, Short Sleeve)
☐ Sports Shirts (i.e. Turtleneck, T-shirt, Polo/Golf)
☐ Flannel or Wool Shirts or Jackets
☐ Sweatshirts
☐ Sweatpants
☐ Sweaters
☐ Suits
☐ Sportcoats
☐ Vests
☐ Jackets (i.e. Windbreaker, All-weather Coat, Parka)
☐ Poncho

- ☐ Raincoat
- ☐ Overcoat
- ☐ Uniforms
- ☐ Coveralls
- ☐ Formal Wear (Tuxedo & Accessories)
- ☐ Jogging or Exercise Outfits
- ☐ Pajamas
- ☐ Bathrobe
- ☐ Belts

- ☐ Suspenders
- ☐ Ties
- ☐ String Ties/Bolos
- ☐ Handkerchiefs
- ☐ Gloves
- ☐ Mufflers
- ☐ Scarves
- ☐ Hats & Caps

9   Bathroom

The bathroom typically contains the things we use to keep ourselves clean, well-groomed, and healthy. This list reflects those essentials, plus adds miscellaneous items that we tend to keep in this room.

Although we tend to keep medicine in our bathrooms, ideally they should be stored in a cool, dark place protected from children and heat. Some medications and first aid supplies are listed here, and you will find an additional list in the "First Aid Kit" in the **Emergency Supplies** section.

Bathroom
- [ ] Hamper
- [ ] Water-saving Devices for Shower, Sink Faucet, & Toilet
- [ ] Drinking Glass(es)
- [ ] Bath Towels
- [ ] Hand Towels
- [ ] Guest Towels
- [ ] Wash Cloths
- [ ] Bath Sponge
- [ ] Bath Mat(s)
- [ ] Soap Dish(es)
- [ ] Bath Soap
- [ ] Face Soap
- [ ] Astringent, Mask & Scrub
- [ ] Facial Sponge
- [ ] Liquid Soap & Pump Dispenser
- [ ] Bubble Bath and/or Bath Oil
- [ ] Shampoo
- [ ] Conditioner
- [ ] Haircolor
- [ ] Shower Caps

- ☐ Razor
- ☐ Razor Blades
- ☐ Shaving Cream
- ☐ Electric Razor
- ☐ Pre-shave
- ☐ After-shave
- ☐ Cologne and/or Perfume
- ☐ Body Lotion
- ☐ Hand Lotion
- ☐ Moisturizer or Other Face Cream
- ☐ Tooth Brushes
- ☐ Toothbrush Holders
- ☐ Toothbrush Covers
- ☐ Tooth Paste
- ☐ Mouthwash
- ☐ Dental Floss
- ☐ Tooth/Mouth Pain Relief Gel (i.e. Anbesol)
- ☐ Orthodontic Aids (i.e. Rubber Bands, Wax, Retainers & Containers, Headgear)
- ☐ Combs
- ☐ Brushes
- ☐ Styling Gel or Mousse
- ☐ Water Bottle with Sprayer
- ☐ Hair Spray
- ☐ Blow Dryer and/or Diffuser
- ☐ Curling Iron
- ☐ Curlers
- ☐ Perm Rods
- ☐ Hair Clips and/or Curl Clips
- ☐ Bobby Pins
- ☐ Barrettes
- ☐ Ponytail Holders
- ☐ Head Bands

- ☐ Misc. Hair Accessories
- ☐ Hair Cutting Scissors
- ☐ Deodorant
- ☐ Bath Powder
- ☐ Petroleum Jelly
- ☐ Lip Balm

Make-up
- ☐ Lipstick
- ☐ Base and/or Cover-up
- ☐ Blush (Powder and/or Cream)
- ☐ Mascara
- ☐ Eyeliner (With Sharpener)
- ☐ Eye Shadow
- ☐ Powder
- ☐ Miscellaneous Cosmetics & Skin Care Products

- ☐ Cotton Balls
- ☐ Cotton Swabs (i.e. Q-tips)
- ☐ Baby Oil
- ☐ Tweezers
- ☐ Nail Scissors
- ☐ Nail Clippers
- ☐ Nail File and/or Emery Boards
- ☐ Cuticle Softener
- ☐ Nail Polish Remover
- ☐ Clear Nail Polish
- ☐ Nail Polish
- ☐ Nail Glue
- ☐ Nail Brush

Feminine Supplies
- ☐ Panty Liners
- ☐ Sanitary Pads
- ☐ Tampons

- ☐ Douche
- ☐ Lubricating Jelly
- ☐ Contraceptives
- ☐ Fever Thermometer (Oral, Rectal, and/or Other)
- ☐ Prescription Medicines (Oral & Topical)
- ☐ Aspirin and/or Similar Medication
- ☐ Cold/Allergy/Sinus Medicine
- ☐ Nasal Spray
- ☐ Eye Drops
- ☐ Ear Drops
- ☐ Anti-diarrhea Medicine
- ☐ Laxative
- ☐ Sleeping Aids
- ☐ Relaxants
- ☐ Rubbing Alcohol
- ☐ Witch Hazel
- ☐ Band-Aids, Assorted Sizes & Shapes
- ☐ Topical Antibacterial Product (i.e Providence Iodine)
- ☐ Bactine or Similar
- ☐ Anti-itch Lotion (i.e. Campho-phenique)
- ☐ Pain Relieving Rub (i.e Ben·Gay)
- ☐ Sunscreen
- ☐ Mosquito Repellant

- ☐ Contact Lens Solution
- ☐ Contact Lens Container
- ☐ Extra Contact Lenses
- ☐ Hand Mirror
- ☐ Vanity Tray
- ☐ Cupboard & Drawer Organizers
- ☐ Shower Caddy
- ☐ Clothing or Towel Hooks (Screw-type or Stick-on)
- ☐ Water Stopper & Plugs
- ☐ Scale for Weighing
- ☐ Toilet Paper
- ☐ Tissues
- ☐ Small Tissue Packets
- ☐ Night Light & Bulbs

Cleaning Supplies
- ☐ Toilet Bowl Brush
- ☐ Pumice
- ☐ Cleansers & Cleaning Products for Toilet, Sink, Shower and/or Bathtub, and Mirror
- ☐ Sponge and/or Cloth
- ☐ Plumber's Helper/Plunger
- ☐ Drain Opener
- ☐ Disinfectant (Liquid or Spray)
- ☐ Air Freshener
- ☐ Potpourri

10 The Laundry Area
(Including Cleaning Equipment & Products)

Not every home has a laundry room or area, but virtually everyone has dirty laundry. Whether or not you have a washer and dryer, you probably need to stock the kinds of things associated with doing the laundry, no matter where you keep them.

Cleaning equipment and products are also listed here because they are at least somewhat related by the nature of their purpose, which is to clean. Remember that when brand names are given, they should not be taken as an endorsement. For ideas on how to make your own cleaning products see the section, **Shopping Green.**

The Laundry Area
- ☐ Laundry Detergent
- ☐ Laundry Soap for Fine Washables (Powder and/or Liquid)
- ☐ Powdered Bleach
- ☐ Liquid Bleach
- ☐ Fabric Softener (Liquid or Sheets)
- ☐ Measuring Cup
- ☐ Stain Remover (Spray or Stick)
- ☐ Laundry Basket(s)
- ☐ Laundry Bag(s)
- ☐ Ironing Board
- ☐ Ironing Board Pad & Cover
- ☐ Iron

- [ ] Iron and/or Ironing Board Caddy
- [ ] Bottled Water
- [ ] Measuring Cup for Ironing Water
- [ ] Spray Bottle
- [ ] Starch and/or Fabric Sizing
- [ ] Clothes Brush
- [ ] Lint Pick-up
- [ ] Spot Remover (Dry Cleaning Type)
- [ ] Wall Tree
- [ ] Hanger Holder, Hooks, Racks & Organizers
- [ ] Clothes Line
- [ ] Clothes Pins
- [ ] Clothes Hangers
- [ ] Fabric Protector Spray for Clothes and Homefurnishings

Cleaning Equipment & Products

- [ ] Bucket and/or Pan
- [ ] Broom
- [ ] Dust Mop
- [ ] Mop
- [ ] Carpet Sweeper
- [ ] Vacuum Cleaner & Attachments
- [ ] Vacuum Cleaner Bags
- [ ] Whisk Broom
- [ ] Dust Pan
- [ ] Cordless Vac (i.e. Dustbuster)
- [ ] Cleaning/Polishing Rags, Assorted Sizes & Textures
- [ ] Sponges
- [ ] Scrub Brushes
- [ ] Feather Duster

- [ ] All-pupose Duster with Extender-type Handle to reach ceilings (i.e. Webster)
- [ ] All-purpose Spray Cleaner
- [ ] All-purpose Cleaner/Water Softener with Trisodium Phosphate (i.e. TSP)
- [ ] Ammonia
- [ ] Oil Soap for Wood
- [ ] Floor Cleaner for Linoleum-type Floors
- [ ] Window Cleaner
- [ ] Degreaser
- [ ] Oven Cleaner
- [ ] Floor Polish and/or Wax (Varies According to Type of Floor)
- [ ] Carpet Spotter
- [ ] Carpet Shampoo
- [ ] Furniture Polish, Wax, and/or Oil
- [ ] Mineral Oil
- [ ] Scratch Remover/Cover-up
- [ ] White Toothpaste
- [ ] Silver Polish
- [ ] Metal Polishes (i.e. Brass, Copper)
- [ ] Shoe/Boot Polishes and Creams
- [ ] Water Repellant Shoe Care Product
- [ ] Jewelry Cleaner
- [ ] Car Care Products (i.e. Shampoo, Wax, Chamois)
- [ ] Mop/Broom Organizer or Other Miscellaneous Organizers, Racks, Hooks, etc.

11 Office & School Supplies

I t is not assumed here that you have an office in your home, although about a third of employed Americans apparently work at home at least part time. Also, students of all ages who do "homework" will use many of the items given in this section.

But, no matter what your employment or student status is, we all have some things that help us organize our lives, communicate with others, and process information.

The office/school inventory is intended for use in an average household. If you do indeed have an in-home office, you will want to add to this list anything specific to the kind of work you do. Also remember that if you have a designated space for an office in your home, you will want to borrow items from other lists in *The Household Inventory Guide* that include furniture and furnishings, books, important papers, and so on.

Office & School Supplies
- ☐ Typewriter & Spare Ribbons & Correcting Ribbons
- ☐ Word Processor & Spare Ribbons & Ink Jets

Computer System
- ☐ Computer
- ☐ Surge Protector
- ☐ Disk Drives
- ☐ Monitor

- ☐ Keyboard
- ☐ Modum
- ☐ Mouse & Pad
- ☐ Printer
- ☐ Scanner
- ☐ Software
- ☐ Diskettes
- ☐ Diskette Files and/or Trays
- ☐ Adding Machine & Paper
- ☐ Calculator & Paper and/or Ribbons

Paper
- ☐ Typing
- ☐ Carbon
- ☐ Computer
- ☐ Copy
- ☐ Scratch
- ☐ Lined Paper Pads
- ☐ Stationery, Assorted
- ☐ Note Cards
- ☐ Letterhead
- ☐ Graph
- ☐ Ledger
- ☐ Binder
- ☐ Notebooks
- ☐ Index Cards
- ☐ Post-it Notes
- ☐ Correction Fluid and/or Tape
- ☐ Business Cards
- ☐ Bank Checks & Deposit Slips
- ☐ Letter Opener
- ☐ Envelopes, Assorted
- ☐ Postage Stamps
- ☐ Post Cards
- ☐ Address Labels and/or Stamp with Pad

- ☐ Mailing Tape
- ☐ Postage Scale
- ☐ Address Books & Directories
- ☐ Phone Book(s)
- ☐ Pens
- ☐ Pencils
- ☐ Erasers
- ☐ Colored Pens, Marking Pens, and/or Pencils
- ☐ Indelible Ink Pen
- ☐ Highlighters
- ☐ Pencil Sharpener
- ☐ Stapler & Staples
- ☐ Staple Gun & Staples
- ☐ Staple Puller
- ☐ Paper Clips
- ☐ Rubber Bands
- ☐ Ruler
- ☐ Protractor
- ☐ Compass
- ☐ Hole Punch
- ☐ Gummed Reinforcements for Holed Paper
- ☐ File Folders
- ☐ File Folder Labels
- ☐ Calendar
- ☐ Appontment Book/Daytimer
- ☐ File Box(es)
- ☐ Card Tray or File
- ☐ Clip Board
- ☐ Binders
- ☐ Binder Indexes
- ☐ Folders
- ☐ Hanging Folders
- ☐ Accordian Folders
- ☐ Scotch Tape

- [ ] Glue
- [ ] Bulletin Board
- [ ] Push Pins
- [ ] Thumb Tacks
- [ ] Desk Pad
- [ ] Desk Organizer
- [ ] Desk Caddy

- [ ] Paper Organizers, Assorted Types & Sizes
- [ ] File Cabinet(s)
- [ ] Record Storage Boxes
- [ ] Fire-safe Security File
- [ ] Brief Case

12 Outdoor Living & Maintenance

T he outdoor areas of our homes can almost be considered as an additional room in the sense that our patios, decks, and gardens offer another space for eating, relaxing, and playing and also for working. They can be an extension of our lifestyles and often require their own furniture, furnishings, and maintenance equipment.

The following lists reflect the work, play, and aesthetics we associate with outdoor living.

Outdoor Living and Maintenance

On or Around the Home

- ☐ Mailbox
- ☐ Address Sign & Number
- ☐ Name Plaque
- ☐ Door Knocker
- ☐ Doormats
- ☐ Windchimes
- ☐ Outdoor Thermometer
- ☐ Weathervane
- ☐ National and/or State Flag & Holder(s)
- ☐ Birdfeeder(s)
- ☐ Birdhouse(s)
- ☐ Birdfeed
- ☐ Garden Lamps
- ☐ Statues
- ☐ Garbage Can(s)
- ☐ Planter Boxes & Liners
- ☐ Pots & Seed-starters

Outdoor Living & Dining

- ☐ Tables (i.e. Picnic Style, Small, Utility Type)
- ☐ Chairs
- ☐ Umbrella

- [ ] Chaise Longues
- [ ] Bench
- [ ] Cushions
- [ ] Hammock
- [ ] Play Equipment
- [ ] Portable Folding Chairs
- [ ] Barbecue
- [ ] Smoker Attachment
- [ ] Rotisserie
- [ ] Drip Pan Liners
- [ ] Ash Catcher
- [ ] Cover
- [ ] Barbecue Table or Cart
- [ ] Fuel (i.e. Charcoal, Propane)
- [ ] Charcoal Funnel
- [ ] Charcoal Companion
- [ ] Lighter Fluid
- [ ] Electric Starter
- [ ] Spray Bottle or Squirt Gun
- [ ] Long-handled Tongs, Spatula, Fork
- [ ] Skewers
- [ ] Basting Brush
- [ ] Grilling Basket
- [ ] Wire Brush to Clean Barbecue
- [ ] Heavy Potholders and/or Mitts
- [ ] Tablecloth(s)
- [ ] Apron
- [ ] Citronella Candles
- [ ] Nonbreakable Glasses & Dishes
- [ ] Paper Plates
- [ ] Paper Plate Holders/Baskets
- [ ] Large Ice Chest
- [ ] Wine Cooling Containers

The Picnic
- [ ] Ground Cloth
- [ ] Picnic Basket
- [ ] Ice Chest
- [ ] "Blue Ice"
- [ ] Utility Knife with Can Opener & Cork Screw
- [ ] Reusable Plastic Cups & Utensils
- [ ] Portable Folding Beach Chairs

Outdoor & Garden Maintenance

- [ ] Broom
- [ ] Dust Pan
- [ ] Rake
- [ ] Hoe
- [ ] Cultivator
- [ ] Shovel
- [ ] Snow Shovel
- [ ] Trowel & Other Digging Tools
- [ ] Trash Bags
- [ ] Ladder
- [ ] Gardening Gloves
- [ ] Gardening Clippers
- [ ] Pruning Tools (i.e. Shears, Saw, Lopper, Pole, Pruner)
- [ ] Hedge Trimmer
- [ ] Lawn Mower
- [ ] Lawn Mower Bag
- [ ] Edger
- [ ] Lawn Aerator
- [ ] Lawn Spreader
- [ ] Weed Eater
- [ ] Leaf Blower
- [ ] Wheelbarrow or Utility Cart

- ☐ Bucket
- ☐ Watering Can
- ☐ Gardening Stakes & Ties
- ☐ Potting Soil
- ☐ Plant Food
- ☐ Fertilizer
- ☐ Fertilizer Spreader
- ☐ Composter
- ☐ Compost Tools
- ☐ Tree Seal
- ☐ Weed Killer
- ☐ Snail & Slug Bait
- ☐ Ant & Insect Poison
- ☐ Garden Hose(s)
- ☐ Hose Reel(s)
- ☐ Decorative Faucet Handles
- ☐ Water Nozzle

- ☐ Sprayer
- ☐ Portable Sprinklers (i.e. Rainbird)
- ☐ Automatic Timer(s) for Sprinklers

Swimming Pool Equipment & Supplies

- ☐ Pool Thermometer
- ☐ Leaf Scoop
- ☐ Brushes (Hand-held & Long Handle)
- ☐ Water-testing Kit
- ☐ Pool Chemicals
- ☐ Toys
- ☐ Floats (i.e. Kick Board, Raft, Life Jackets, Water Wings)

13 Storage

I. Fibber McGee's Closet & Spare Cupboards & Drawers
II. The Garage, Basement, Attic & Storage Shed

S torage covers a lot of ter-
ritory, both literally and
figuratively. It refers to the
kinds of spaces where we
keep things that aren't in constant use. It includes all sorts of
things that are not particularly related to other items on the list,
except that they are all things that can be put away.

Some of the items here appear on other lists but are included
in this section also because they are often stored out of sight and
not necessarily in the room where they are mostly associated.
Table leaves and pads, for instance, are not usually in use as part
of the dining room table in that room. More often than not,
they are in a closet somewhere else awaiting a dinner party.

Some of the items listed here are whole categories in themselves and have their own separate sections. When that is the
case, the items will be preceded by an asterisk and followed by a
note in parentheses directing you to that section. For example,
*Luggage & Other Travel Items will say, (See **Travel**.)

This section is divided into two parts. Although certain items
are somewhat arbitrarily placed in one part or the other, the idea
is that we tend to keep some of our things in closets, cupboards,
and drawers, while we store others in larger spaces (if we have
them) like a garage, basement, attic, or shed.

I. Fibber McGee's Closet & Spare Cupboards & Drawers

- ☐ Extra Bedding & Pillows
- ☐ Extra Towels & Miscellaneous Linens
- ☐ Beach Towels
- ☐ Sleeping Bags
- ☐ Backpacks
- ☐ Table Leaves & Pads
- ☐ Portable Sewing Machine

Sewing Kit
- ☐ Pin Cushion
- ☐ Straight Pins
- ☐ Needles
- ☐ Needle Threader
- ☐ Safety Pins
- ☐ Sewing Machine Needles & Oil
- ☐ Bobbins
- ☐ Thread, Assorted
- ☐ Scissors
- ☐ Pinking Shears
- ☐ Embroidery Scissors
- ☐ Thimble
- ☐ Crochet Hook
- ☐ Seam Ripper
- ☐ Tailor's Chalk
- ☐ Measuring Tape
- ☐ Patches
- ☐ Indelible Ink Marking Pen
- ☐ Name Labels
- ☐ Hooks & Eyes
- ☐ Snaps
- ☐ Elastic
- ☐ Extra Buttons
- ☐ Seam Binding

- ☐ Material Scraps
- ☐ Humidifier/Vaporizer
- ☐ Heating Pad
- ☐ Ice Pack
- ☐ Fly Swatter
- ☐ Yard Stick
- ☐ Light Bulbs, Assorted
- ☐ Flashlights
- ☐ Candles
- ☐ Candle Holders
- ☐ Batteries, Assorted
- ☐ Battery Tester
- ☐ Battery Recharger
- ☐ Extension Cords
- ☐ Plug Extenders
- ☐ Automatic Light Timers
- ☐ String
- ☐ Twine
- ☐ Rope
- ☐ Wire
- ☐ Bungee Cords

Tape
- ☐ Scotch
- ☐ Mailing
- ☐ Strapping
- ☐ Masking
- ☐ Duct
- ☐ Paste

Glue
- ☐ Mucilage
- ☐ All-purpose
- ☐ Household Cement
- ☐ Wood Glue
- ☐ Glue Stick
- ☐ Super Glue

- [ ] Picture Hooks & Holders
- [ ] Tacks
- [ ] Umbrellas
- [ ] Binoculars
- [ ] Camera
- [ ] Film
- [ ] Photograph Albums
- [ ] Containers, "Frogs" & Oasis for Plants & Flowers
- [ ] Watering Can with Spout for House Plants
- [ ] Boxes, Assorted Sizes to Hold Miscellaneous Odds & Ends
- [ ] Gift Boxes, Assorted Sizes & Shapes
- [ ] Gift Wrapping Paper
- [ ] Tissue Paper
- [ ] Ribbons & Bows
- [ ] Gift Cards and/or Tags
- [ ] Greeting Cards
- [ ] Coupon Organizer
- [ ] Maps
- [ ] Magnifying Glass
- [ ] Spare Reading Glasses
- [ ] Eye Glass Cord or Chain
- [ ] Eye Glass Repair Kit
- [ ] Sun Glasses
- [ ] Lining Material for Shelves, Drawers & Cupboards
- [ ] Sachet for Drawers
- [ ] Color Palette or Swatches (for those who have had their colors done)
- [ ] Miscellaneous Decorative Items & Bric-a-Brac
- [ ] Ashtrays

- [ ] Door Stops
- [ ] Fireproof Container (i.e. Safe)
- [ ] *Hobby Items & Collections (See"The Arts,Hobbies & Collections")
- [ ] Costumes

II. The Garage, Basement, Attic & Shed
Tools
- [ ] Tool Box
- [ ] Measuring Tape
- [ ] Level
- [ ] Hammer (Claw)
- [ ] Screwdrivers (Regular & Phillips,Assorted Sizes)
- [ ] Pliers (Needlenose & Others)
- [ ] Wirecutter
- [ ] Crescent Wrench
- [ ] Allen Wrench Set
- [ ] Chisel
- [ ] Nail Set
- [ ] Electrician's Tape
- [ ] Duct Tape
- [ ] Wire
- [ ] Hacksaw
- [ ] Crowbar
- [ ] Razor
- [ ] Scraper
- [ ] Utility Knife
- [ ] Putty Knife
- [ ] C-clamps
- [ ] Socket Set
- [ ] Drill & Drill Bits
- [ ] Carpenter's Square

- [ ] Sandpaper
- [ ] Epoxy Cement
- [ ] Heavy-duty Extension Cord
- [ ] Assortment of Nails, Nuts, Screws, Woodscrews, & Washers
- [ ] Electric Tools (i.e. Screwdriver, Sander, Drill, Jigsaw, etc.)
- [ ] Ladder
- [ ] Handtruck and/or Dolly
- [ ] Saw Horses
- [ ] Fire Extinguisher (A-B-C Rating, Halon-free)
- [ ] Filters for Furnace and/or Air Conditioner
- [ ] *Cleaning Equipment & Products (See **The Laundry Area**)

Miscellaneous Home Maintenance Supplies

- [ ] Paint
- [ ] Paint Thinner
- [ ] Paint Brushes
- [ ] Paint Gun
- [ ] Mortar
- [ ] Caulking
- [ ] Patching Plaster
- [ ] Spackling
- [ ] Carpenter's Wood Filler
- [ ] Stipple
- [ ] Sandpaper

- [ ] Steel Wool
- [ ] Abrasive Nylon Pads
- [ ] Household Oil
- [ ] Squeak Stopper (i.e. WD-40)
- [ ] *Car Equipment & Supplies (See **The Car**)
- [ ] *Camping & Backpacking Equipment (See **Camping & Backpacking**)
- [ ] *Sporting Goods & Exercise Equipment (See **Recreation, Sports & Exercise**)
- [ ] Plant Food, Fertilizer & Potting Soil
- [ ] *Luggage & Other Travel Items (See **Travel**)
- [ ] Firewood
- [ ] Kindling
- [ ] Firewood Carrier
- [ ] Trouble Light
- [ ] Oil Lamps
- [ ] Lamp Oil
- [ ] *Emergency & First Aid Supplies (See **Emergency Supplies**)
- [ ] Convalescent Equipment
- [ ] Storage Oraganizers, Caddies, Drawers, Baskets, Racks, S Racks, Hooks & Clips,Peg Board,Parts Bins, etc.
- [ ] *Hobby Items & Collections (See **The Arts, Hobbies & Collections**)

14 Emergency Supplies

S ince the Loma Prieta earthquake in 1989, there has been a growing consciousness and concern among the people of California about being prepared for "the big one." But all of us, no matter where we live, are subject to threats of one kind of disaster or another. We are advised to keep enough emergency supplies on hand to last us a few days in case we are left to our own devices. The following list is an attempt to meet that need.

Included here is a first aid kit. Items in the kit are intended to be kept together as an important part of all the emergency supplies. But they also include many of the everyday kinds of things that we usually keep in our bathrooms and kitchens. You may want to put together a separate first aid kit to keep in your car or to take on trips.

Water, canned or packaged foods, and medications should be checked periodically to make sure that dates haven't expired.

Getting your emergency supplies together is a good time to think about the most important tasks to do and which people to contact after a personal diaster, both for practical reasons and to relieve anxiety.

Emergency Supplies

- [ ] Container(s) to Hold Emergency Supplies
- [ ] Bottled Water (2 Qts. to 2 Gals. Per Person Per Day)
- [ ] Sterilized, Purified Pouches of Water
- [ ] Canned Juices

Food (At Least 5 Day Supply Per Person)
- [ ] Packaged, Canned, Dehydrated Assortment
- [ ] Food Bars
- [ ] Food for Infants and/or Pets

Cooking & Eating Utensils
- [ ] Barbecue or Camp Stove
- [ ] Fuel
- [ ] Matches in Waterproof Container
- [ ] Pot or Pan
- [ ] Stirring/Serving Spoon
- [ ] Sharp Knife
- [ ] Portable Can Opener
- [ ] Nonbreakable Plates, Bowls, and Cups
- [ ] Knives, Forks, and Spoons
- [ ] Paper Towels
- [ ] Heavy-duty Aluminum Foil
- [ ] Wash Pan
- [ ] Dish Soap
- [ ] Flashlight and Extra Batteries
- [ ] Portable Radio & Extra Batteries
- [ ] Whistle (To call for help)
- [ ] Tools (i.e. Wrench to turn off utilities, Hammer, Pliers, Screwdrivers, Ax, Crowbar)

Information
- [ ] Map of Area
- [ ] Directions to Local Hospitals & Emergency Relief Centers
- [ ] Telephone Numbers of Local Police, Fire Department, and Hospital
- [ ] Contact Person (Preferably out of state) with whom family members can check

Sanitary Supplies
- [ ] Bucket
- [ ] Large Plastic Bags with Ties
- [ ] Newspapers
- [ ] Toilet Paper
- [ ] Disinfectant
- [ ] Deodorizer
- [ ] Premoistened Disposable Towels
- [ ] Feminine & Infant Supplies
- [ ] Bar Soap
- [ ] Shampoo
- [ ] Toothpaste
- [ ] Toothbrushes
- [ ] Plastic Sheeting
- [ ] Staple Gun
- [ ] Dust Masks
- [ ] Work Gloves
- [ ] Duct Tape
- [ ] Fire Extinguisher (A-B-C Rating, Halon-free)
- [ ] Paper, Pencils, Pens
- [ ] Scissors

☐ Candles

☐ Blankets (Insulated, All-weather Thermal)

☐ Change of Clothing (Include Rain Gear)

☐ Sturdy Shoes

☐ Cash (Small Bills & Change for Telephone)

☐ Coil of 1/2" Rope

☐ Books, Magazines, Games, Toys

First Aid Kit

☐ First Aid Instruction Handbook

☐ Writing Materials (i.e. Paper, Pencils, Pens)

☐ Prescription and/or Other Special Medicine

☐ Pain Relief Medication (i.e. Aspirin, Ibuprofen)

☐ Scissors

☐ Tweezers

☐ Rubbing Alcohol Preps

☐ Antibacterial Solution (i.e. Providine Iodine)

☐ Baking Soda

☐ Table Salt

☐ Antacids

☐ Cough Mixture

☐ Throat Lozenges

☐ Diarrhea Medication

☐ Laxative

☐ Ear Drops

☐ Toothache Remedy

☐ Motion Sickness Tablets (For nausea)

☐ Topical Ointment

☐ Box of Plastic Strips (i.e. Band-Aids), Assorted Sizes

☐ Clean Sheet (To use for bandages)

☐ Roll of Adhesive Tape (2" Wide)

☐ Sterile Gauze

☐ 4" x 4" Sterile Dressing Pads

☐ Sterile Cotton

☐ ABD or Sanitary Pads

☐ 24" Ace Bandage Wrap

☐ Splints (18" Wooden)

☐ Cotton Swabs

☐ Safety Pins, Assorted Sizes

☐ Fever Thermometer(s)

☐ Eyedropper

☐ Water Purification Materials

☐ Collapsible or Paper Cups

☐ Waterproof Matches

☐ 2 Quick Cold Packs

☐ Resealable, Waterproof Bags

15 Infants & Toddlers

Many of the items listed here are used by both infants and toddlers, while others are best suited for either one or the other. Although they are are fairly well interspersed, there are more infant items toward the beginning of the list and more toddler things at the end.

Infants & Toddlers
- Crib with Waterproof Mattress
- Bumper Pads
- Waterproof Mattress Pads
- Fitted Sheets
- Blankets/Quilts/Comforters
- Dressing Table
- Chest of Drawers
- Portacrib
- Travel Sleeper & Bedding
- Cradle/Bassinet
- Playpen & Pad
- Baby Bath
- Reclining Infant Seat
- Auto Safety Seat
- Collapsible Stroller
- Pram/Baby Carriage
- Baby Carrier (Back or Front) for Parents
- Highchair or Feeding Table
- Diapers
- Waterproof Pants
- Diaper Stacker
- Diaper Bag
- Diaper Pail & Deodorizers
- Lap Pads

Layette Items
- ☐ Receiving Blankets
- ☐ Washcloths
- ☐ Hooded Towels
- ☐ After-bath Bags
- ☐ Snapside Shirts
- ☐ Diaper Covers
- ☐ Gowns
- ☐ Bodysuits
- ☐ Stretchies
- ☐ Coming Home Outfit
- ☐ Bunting
- ☐ Coveralls
- ☐ Pullover Shirts
- ☐ Bibs
- ☐ Booties & Baby Shoes
- ☐ Socks
- ☐ Cap or Bonnet
- ☐ Sweater Sets

☐ Sterilizer with Bottle Nurser Set
☐ Breast Pump Set
☐ Food Grinder
☐ Food Tray
☐ Nonbreakable Bowls
☐ Nonbreakable Spillproof Cup with Lid
☐ Baby Spoons
☐ Pacifiers (Orthodontic)

Nursery Accessories
- ☐ Baby Monitor
- ☐ Mobile
- ☐ Crib Skirt
- ☐ Canopy
- ☐ Crib Pillow
- ☐ Crib Toys
- ☐ Toy Chest
- ☐ Hamper
- ☐ Nursery Scale
- ☐ Lamp
- ☐ Switchplate
- ☐ Wallhangings/Pictures/Plaques

☐ Stuffed Animals
☐ Rattle
☐ Teething Ring/Toys
☐ Bath Toys
☐ Cloth Books

Personal Care Items
- ☐ Soap
- ☐ Antibacterial Cleanser
- ☐ Shampoo
- ☐ Oil
- ☐ Lotion
- ☐ Diaper Rash Ointment
- ☐ Premoistened Towelettes and/or Diaper Wipes
- ☐ Diaper Liners
- ☐ Nail Scissors
- ☐ Hair Brush & Comb
- ☐ Themometer (Rectal and/or Underarm)
- ☐ Nasal Syringe
- ☐ Cotton Balls
- ☐ Cotton Swabs
- ☐ Tissues
- ☐ Baby Laundry Detergent

☐ Baby Record Book
☐ Photograph Albums
☐ Parenting Books
☐ Walkers/Jumpers/Exercisers
☐ Potty Training Chair/Seat

- ☐ Bath Toys
- ☐ Step Chair
- ☐ Booster Seat
- ☐ Child Size Table & Chairs
- ☐ Humidifier/Vaporizer
- ☐ Books/Picture Books
- ☐ Toys
- ☐ Lightweight Balls (i.e. Nerf, Whiffle)

Safety Equipment
- ☐ Guardrail
- ☐ Expandable Security Gates
- ☐ Electrical Outlet Plugs or Guards
- ☐ Door Knob Covers
- ☐ Door Locks
- ☐ Cabinet Door Locks and/or Safety Catches
- ☐ Medicine Cabinet Locks
- ☐ Drawer Stops
- ☐ Window Safety Locks

- ☐ Child Safety & Emergency Book

Clothing
- ☐ Socks
- ☐ Shoes
- ☐ Training Pants
- ☐ Underpants
- ☐ Undershirts
- ☐ Tights
- ☐ Pajamas
- ☐ Sleepers
- ☐ Coveralls
- ☐ Shirts/Blouses
- ☐ Dresses
- ☐ Sweaters
- ☐ Sweatshirts
- ☐ Jackets
- ☐ Caps/Hats/Bonnets
- ☐ Snowsuit
- ☐ Raingear

16   Kids' Stuff

M ost of the things on this list apply primarily to young children, including older toddlers. Other items, like video games, balls, and a train set, may appeal to children of all ages.

School-age and older children don't have a separate list of their own because most of their belongings can be found in the regular sections. School supplies, for instance, are included in the **Office & School Supply** section, and clothes are covered in the **Bedroom**, along with what adults wear. They may also have a number of items listed in the **Recreation, Sports & Exercise** section.

Kids' Stuff
- ☐ Child-size Furniture (i.e. Table & Chairs, Rocking Chairs)
- ☐ Night Light
- ☐ Books
- ☐ Stuffed Animals
- ☐ Dolls
- ☐ Doll Accessories (i.e. Clothes, Furniture, House, Tea Set)
- ☐ Puppets
- ☐ Balls
- ☐ Frisbee
- ☐ Stacking & Shape-sorting Toys
- ☐ Building Toys (i.e Blocks, Legos, Lincoln Logs, Tinkertoys)
- ☐ Platform Toys (i.e. Play Family, Post Office)

- ☐ Jack-in-the-Box
- ☐ Top
- ☐ Toy Cars & Trucks
- ☐ Puzzles
- ☐ Color Forms
- ☐ Magnets (i.e. Alphabet)

Art Supplies

- ☐ Paper, Assorted
- ☐ Scissors
- ☐ Paste
- ☐ Glue
- ☐ Crayons
- ☐ Watercolors & Brushes
- ☐ Fingerpaint
- ☐ Easel
- ☐ Smock
- ☐ Clay
- ☐ Playdough
- ☐ Musical Instruments
- ☐ Phonograph & Records
- ☐ Tape Recorder & Cassette Tapes
- ☐ Board Games
- ☐ Electronic Games (i.e. Nintendo, Gameboy)
- ☐ Video Games
- ☐ Model Kits
- ☐ Kites
- ☐ Push Toys (i.e. Shopping Cart, Lawn Mower)

- ☐ Pull Toys (Wagon, Animals)
- ☐ Rocking Horse
- ☐ Riding Toys without Pedals
- ☐ Miniature House & Accessories
- ☐ Train Set
- ☐ Big Wheel or Other Riding Toys
- ☐ Tricycle
- ☐ Bicycle & Training Wheels
- ☐ Bike Accessories (i.e. Basket, Bell or Horn)
- ☐ Scooter
- ☐ Skate Board
- ☐ Roller Skates and/or Roller Blades
- ☐ Inflatable Swimming Pool
- ☐ Swing Set
- ☐ Slide
- ☐ Climbing Toys
- ☐ Sand Box
- ☐ Sand Toys (i.e. Bucket, Shovel)
- ☐ Snow Toys (i.e.Sled, Inner Tube)
- ☐ Travel Activity Games & Books
- ☐ Backpack
- ☐ Lunch Box and/or Lined Bag

17   Pet Supplies

Pets are so important to us that they are like family members. We look out for them and care for them almost as if they are our children. The following list of supplies will provide you with what you need for their feeding, grooming, safety, and overall well-being.

Pet Supplies
- ☐ Food & Water Dishes
- ☐ Placemat
- ☐ Pet Food
- ☐ Snack Food
- ☐ Automatic Pet Feeder
- ☐ Food Containers
- ☐ Vitamins & Minerals
- ☐ Skin or Other Supplements
- ☐ Medicine (Oral and/or Topical)
- ☐ Dental Care Products
- ☐ Things to Chew
- ☐ Shampoo
- ☐ Conditioner
- ☐ Sink Shower
- ☐ Pet Brush
- ☐ Pet Comb
- ☐ Nail Clippers & File
- ☐ Flea & Tick Powder, Spray, or Collar
- ☐ Collar, Tags & Reflector
- ☐ Choke Collar
- ☐ Small Dog Harness
- ☐ Leash
- ☐ Chain or Other Tether
- ☐ Portable Enclosure
- ☐ Invisible Fence with Receiver Collar
- ☐ Security Gate

- ☐ Car Barrier
- ☐ Pet Door
- ☐ "Pooper Scooper"
- ☐ Pet Hair Pick-up
- ☐ Dog Whistle
- ☐ House/Cage/Tank/Bowl
- ☐ Portable Kennel
- ☐ Bed/Basket & Cushion
- ☐ Litter Box with Liner, Litter & Scoop
- ☐ Scratching Post
- ☐ Hamster Cage with Exercise Wheel
- ☐ Bedding Material for Hamsters, Gerbils & Pet Mice
- ☐ Bird Cage with Perches & Perch Cleaner

- ☐ Bird Bottle & Feeder
- ☐ Aquarium
- ☐ Aquarium Accessories (i.e. Air Pump, Light, Heater, Filter, Air Valve, Aerator Bar, Net, Airline Tubing, Thermometer, Filter Floss, Activated Carbon, Plants, Ornamental Items)
- ☐ Terrarium & Moss
- ☐ Reptile Cage Carpet, Rocks & Rock Warmer
- ☐ Toys
- ☐ Pet Literature (i.e. American Kennel Club Books)
- ☐ Medical Records
- ☐ Pedigree Papers

18 Recreation, Sports & Exercise

This section lists a wide range of recreational, sports, and exercise activities and their basic equipment. Most households likely include one or more of these categories but certainly not all, or even most.

Some of the groupings may appear sparse, but that is intentional. Instead of listing every piece of clothing or equipment for every activity or sport, I have listed some generic items at the top. These can be added to appropriate subsections when needed. Take the category football, for instance. Theoretically, all you need to play is a ball and some players. But if you are on a team, you obviously need a number of the generic items, including a uniform and shoes with cleats.

Some kind of case or bag is useful, or even necessary, for a number of the listings. If that's true for your particular sport or activity, just add that to your list in this mix and match section.

Recreation, Sports, & Exercise

Generic Items That Apply or Can Be Adapted to Various Activites

- ☐ Hats, Caps, Helmets & Visors
- ☐ Clothes & Uniforms
- ☐ Raingear
- ☐ Shoes & Boots
- ☐ Shoe Repair Supplies (i.e. Shoe-Goo)

- [ ] Gloves
- [ ] Goggles
- [ ] Carrying Case
- [ ] Sports Bag
- [ ] Hip Pack
- [ ] Sweatband
- [ ] Wristband
- [ ] Kneeguard
- [ ] Elbowguard
- [ ] Mouth Guard
- [ ] Sweat Towel
- [ ] Water Bottle
- [ ] Air Pump
- [ ] Instructional & Rule Books or Manuals

Archery
- [ ] Bows
- [ ] Arrows
- [ ] Quiver
- [ ] Target

Badminton
- [ ] Raquets
- [ ] Birdies
- [ ] Net

Baseball/Softball
- [ ] Bat
- [ ] Ball
- [ ] Mitt

Basketball
- [ ] Ball
- [ ] Backboard with Hoop & Net

Bicycling
- [ ] Bicycle
- [ ] Cable or Chain & Lock
- [ ] Bike Tool Set

- [ ] Basket
- [ ] Training Wheels for Beginners
- [ ] Rack

Billiards/Pool
- [ ] Table
- [ ] Balls
- [ ] Cue Sticks
- [ ] Bridge Head
- [ ] Triangle
- [ ] Chalk
- [ ] Table Brush
- [ ] Table Cover
- [ ] Cue Rack

Bowling
- [ ] Ball
- [ ] Resin/Powder

Boxing
- [ ] Gloves
- [ ] Punching Bag Set

Croquet
- [ ] Mallets
- [ ] Balls
- [ ] Goal Stakes
- [ ] Hoops

Darts
- [ ] Darts
- [ ] Dart Board

Exercise Equipment
- [ ] Floor Mat
- [ ] Exercise Bike
- [ ] Treadmill
- [ ] Rower
- [ ] Trampoline
- [ ] Wrist & Ankle Weights

Fishing
- ☐ Rod
- ☐ Reel
- ☐ Tackle Box
- ☐ Hooks
- ☐ Fishing Lines
- ☐ Weights
- ☐ Bait and/or Lures or Flies
- ☐ Net
- ☐ Knife
- ☐ Fish Scaler
- ☐ Waders

Football
- ☐ Ball

Golf
- ☐ Clubs
- ☐ Bag
- ☐ Balls
- ☐ Tees
- ☐ Ball Markers
- ☐ Green Repair Tools
- ☐ Cart
- ☐ Club Covers
- ☐ Ball Retriever
- ☐ Umbrella

Horseshoes
- ☐ Horseshoes
- ☐ Pegs

Hunting/Shooting
- ☐ Gun
- ☐ Ammunition
- ☐ Targets
- ☐ Gun Cleaning Kit
- ☐ Gun Case
- ☐ Hunting Knife

Ping Pong/Table Tennis
- ☐ Table
- ☐ Net
- ☐ Paddles
- ☐ Balls

Raquetball
- ☐ Raquet
- ☐ Balls
- ☐ Raquet Cover

Skiing
- ☐ Skis
- ☐ Poles
- ☐ Boots
- ☐ Boot Carrier
- ☐ After-ski Boots
- ☐ Ski Rack

Soccer
- ☐ Ball

Swimming & Related
- ☐ Lifejacket
- ☐ Fins
- ☐ Water Socks
- ☐ Diving Mask/Goggles
- ☐ Ear Plugs
- ☐ Nose Plug
- ☐ Snorkel
- ☐ Wet Suit
- ☐ Kickboard
- ☐ Raft
- ☐ Water Skis
- ☐ Scuba Equipment
- ☐ Water Toys, Games, & Floats
- ☐ Swimmer's Towel/Chamois
- ☐ Beach Towels

Tennis
- ☐ Raquet
- ☐ Balls
- ☐ Raquet Cover and/or Press

Tetherball
- ☐ Tetherball Set

Volleyball
- ☐ Ball
- ☐ Net

Weightlifting
- ☐ Barbell/Dumbell Set
- ☐ Weight Bench

Miscellaneous
- ☐ Jump Rope
- ☐ Roller Skates
- ☐ Roller Blades
- ☐ Ice Skates
- ☐ Skateboard

18 Travel

W hat you will need from the travel list depends on what kind of trips you take and how long you are gone from home. Some of the items listed you would probably take with you on even the shortest of trips, such as luggage and a cosmetic bag or shaving kit. Other items like a currency converter and foreign language dictionaries you would only need if you are traveling out of the country.

You may want to borrow ideas from the next section, **Camping & Backpacking**, to add to your travel list. There you will find things like a sleeping bag, towels, and eating utensils, which are not included here. Also not included here are many of the personal items normally found in the bathroom with which we stuff our cosmetic bags and shaving kits, so you may want to check that list, too.

Travel

Luggage

- ☐ Garment Bag
- ☐ 28" Pullman
- ☐ 26" Pullman
- ☐ Carry-on
- ☐ Tote Bag
- ☐ Train Case
- ☐ Backpack
- ☐ Lightweight Folding Suitcase to Pack

- [ ] Fanny Pack
- [ ] Luggage Tags
- [ ] Luggage Carrier (With Wheels & Cords)
- [ ] Cosmetic Bag
- [ ] Shaving Kit
- [ ] Soapdish with Soap
- [ ] Travel Size Toiletries (i.e. Toothpaste, Shampoo & Conditioner, Shaving Cream, Cologne, etc.)
- [ ] Small Plastic Containers for Body Lotion, Moisturizer, etc.
- [ ] Toothbrush Cover
- [ ] Pill Containers
- [ ] Shower Cap
- [ ] Swimmers's Towel/Chamois
- [ ] Towelettes
- [ ] Small Tissue Packets
- [ ] Small Blow Dryer
- [ ] Mirror
- [ ] Suction Sink Stopper
- [ ] Utility Knife with Can Opener & Wine Opener
- [ ] Cutting Board
- [ ] Folding Cup
- [ ] Heating Cord
- [ ] Travel Flasks
- [ ] Ice Pack

- [ ] Jewelry Case
- [ ] Camera Case
- [ ] Film Shield
- [ ] Travel Iron or Steamer
- [ ] Clothes Hangers
- [ ] Clothes Pins
- [ ] Portable Clothesline
- [ ] Small Sewing Kit
- [ ] Spot Remover
- [ ] Laundry Soap (Regular & for Fine Fabrics)
- [ ] Lint Pick-up
- [ ] Laundry Bag
- [ ] Shoe Covers
- [ ] Travel Alarm Clock
- [ ] Folding Umbrella
- [ ] Lightweight Folding Raingear
- [ ] Small Size Travel Games & Playing Cards
- [ ] Money Belt

International Travel Items
- [ ] Foreign Language Dictionaries
- [ ] Converter
- [ ] Adaptor Plugs
- [ ] Currency Converter
- [ ] Calculator
- [ ] Drinking Water Tablets or Solution

20 Camping & Backpacking

This section is at least minimumly interchangable with the previous section on travel, but the focus here is on outdoor trips and their requisite supplies. Some of the items assume being outdoors in inclement weather and may not apply if your outings happen to be in a location with a warm climate.

Backpackers who also camp will need to be more selective in deciding what to pack than regular campers, considering the limited amount of supplies one is able to carry in a backpack.

Camping & Backpacking
- [ ] Backpack
- [ ] Sleeping Bag
- [ ] Pillow & Pillow Case
- [ ] Air Mattress & Pump or Foam Mat
- [ ] Groundcloth and/or Tarp
- [ ] Cot
- [ ] Tent & Stakes
- [ ] Lantern & Fuel
- [ ] Cookstove & Fuel
- [ ] Charcoal
- [ ] Newspaper
- [ ] Matches and/or Butane Lighter
- [ ] Ice Chest

Cook Kit
- [ ] Stewing Pot(s) & Lid(s)
- [ ] Frying Pan
- [ ] Coffee Pot
- [ ] Unbreakable Plates & Bowls

- ☐ Unbreakable Cups
- ☐ Knives, Forks, & Spoons
- ☐ Sharp Knife
- ☐ Can Opener
- ☐ Cutting Board
- ☐ Thermos
- ☐ Dishpan
- ☐ Soap (i.e. Dish, Laundry, Bath Soap & Covered Soap Dish)
- ☐ DishTowels
- ☐ Two-sided Sponge with Scouring Pad
- ☐ Tin Foil
- ☐ Food Wrap
- ☐ Food Storage Bags
- ☐ Trash Bags
- ☐ Paper Towels, Napkins, & Toilet Paper
- ☐ Rope (i.e. Nylon Utility Cord or 50 Foot Nylon Parachute Cord)
- ☐ Bungee Cords
- ☐ Clothespins
- ☐ Ax
- ☐ Small Broom or Rake
- ☐ Shovel
- ☐ Duct Tape
- ☐ Pocket Knife
- ☐ A Few Small Handtools
- ☐ Flashlight & Extra Batteries
- ☐ Portable Radio & Extra Batteries
- ☐ Canteen
- ☐ Compass
- ☐ Whistle

- ☐ Tennis Shoes
- ☐ Hiking Boots
- ☐ Wool Socks & Sock Liners
- ☐ Long Underwear
- ☐ Wool Hat
- ☐ Wool Gloves
- ☐ Brimmed Hat or Visor
- ☐ Bandana
- ☐ Waterproof Rainjacket
- ☐ Assorted Clothes to Layer According to Weather
- ☐ Belt or Suspenders
- ☐ Dark Glasses (100% Ultraviolet Ray Blockage)
- ☐ Sunscreen
- ☐ Insect Repellant
- ☐ Lip Protector
- ☐ Vitamins and/or Prescription Medicine
- ☐ First Aid Kit, Including Band-Aids & Moleskin
- ☐ Needle & Thread
- ☐ Personal Items (i.e. Toothbrush, Toothpaste, Comb, etc.)
- ☐ Towels & Washcloths
- ☐ Beach Towel
- ☐ Beach Mat

Miscellaneous Items

- ☐ Camera & Film
- ☐ Reading Material
- ☐ Cards & Games
- ☐ Notebook, Pen, & Pencil
- ☐ Envelopes & Stamps
- ☐ Small Musical Instrument

- ☐ Art Supplies
- ☐ Fishing Equipment
- ☐ Bicycle, Helmet, & Water Bottle

- ☐ Recreational Equipment (i.e. Frisbee, Balls, etc.)

21 **Books** (Fiction & Nonfiction)

T his section will be especially helpful to those of you who have lost the contents of your homes, including your reading material. Although most of the lost books won't or can't be replaced, the following list is fairly comprehensive in terms of the categories of books published. It is provided as a memory aid to help remind you of the kinds of books that are missing and those you will want to have when you begin to restock your bookshelves.

Obviously, you will have to prioritize according to your needs and available income. But books commonly found in many households include cook books, reference books (like a dictionary, thesaurus, set of encyclopedias, and a medical guide), work-related books, how-to books (such as guides to resume writing, household maintenance, gardening, parenting), novels, a "coffee table" book, and religious books such as a *Bible*.

Incidentally, Oakland-Berkeley fire survivors were offered free replacement of their encyclopedias by at least two groups (*World Book Encyclopedia and Encyclopedia Britannica*) if their sets had been purchased within the past five years.

Books (Fiction & Nonfiction)

- [ ] Adventure
- [ ] Agriculture/Horticulture
- [ ] Americana
- [ ] Animals
- [ ] Anthropology/Archaeology
- [ ] Autobiography
- [ ] Biography
- [ ] Business/Economics
- [ ] Catalogs
- [ ] Child Guidance/Parenting
- [ ] Communication
- [ ] Community/Public Affairs
- [ ] Computers/Electronics
- [ ] Consumer Affairs
- [ ] Cooking/Foods/Nutrition
- [ ] Counseling/Career Guidance
- [ ] Crafts
- [ ] Educational
- [ ] Entertainment/Games
- [ ] Ethnic
- [ ] Fantasy
- [ ] Fashion/Beauty
- [ ] Feminism
- [ ] Film/Cinema/Stage
- [ ] Gardening
- [ ] Gay/Lesbian
- [ ] General Nonfiction
- [ ] Geography
- [ ] Government/Politics
- [ ] Health/Medicine
- [ ] Historical Fiction
- [ ] History
- [ ] Hobby
- [ ] Horror
- [ ] How-to
- [ ] Humanities
- [ ] Humor
- [ ] Juvenile Books
- [ ] Labor/Management
- [ ] Language & Literature
- [ ] Law
- [ ] Literary Criticism
- [ ] Mainstream/Contemporary Fiction
- [ ] Marine Subjects
- [ ] Men's Issues & Subjects
- [ ] Military/War
- [ ] Money/Finance
- [ ] Music & Dance
- [ ] Mystery
- [ ] Novels
- [ ] Nature & Environment
- [ ] Philosophy
- [ ] Photography
- [ ] Picture Books
- [ ] Plays
- [ ] Poetry
- [ ] Psychology
- [ ] Real Estate
- [ ] Recreation
- [ ] Reference
- [ ] Regional
- [ ] Religion
- [ ] Romance
- [ ] Scholarly
- [ ] Science Fiction
- [ ] Science/Technology
- [ ] Self-help
- [ ] Short Story Collections
- [ ] Social Sciences
- [ ] Sociology

- ☐ Spiritual (New Age)
- ☐ Sports
- ☐ Technical
- ☐ Textbook
- ☐ Transportation

- ☐ Travel
- ☐ Western
- ☐ Women's Studies/Issues
- ☐ World Affairs
- ☐ Young Adult

22 The Arts, Hobbies & Collections

T he arts generally refer to art, literature, music, and drama. This section will not do justice to professionals in these areas. Nor will it be of much help to collectors of fine art. It is intended rather for those who enjoy certain activities outside of regular work or school hours.

One definition of the word hobby is that it is something that a person likes to do or study in his or her spare time–a favorite pastime or avocation. Since there are almost endless possibilities here, this section can never be considered to be totally complete.

As for collections, my sister once claimed that if you have three of anything, you have a collection. That made me a collector of old brooms at the time. The following lists are an attempt to mention some of the most common things that people do, study, or collect.

The Arts, Hobbies & Collections
Hobbies

- ☐ Photography
- ☐ Painting, Sketching & Drawing
- ☐ Calligraphy
- ☐ Crafts
- ☐ Sewing
- ☐ Handcrafts (i.e. Knitting, Crocheting, Embroidery, Needlepoint, Weaving, Quilting, Macrame)
- ☐ Jewelry Making
- ☐ Flower Arranging
- ☐ Sculpting
- ☐ Pottery/Ceramics
- ☐ Stained Glass Making
- ☐ Music (Playing Musical Instruments)
- ☐ Home Decorating
- ☐ Furniture Refinishing
- ☐ Woodworking/Carpentry
- ☐ Home Improvements
- ☐ Car Repair
- ☐ Electronics
- ☐ Model Trains
- ☐ Model Building
- ☐ Gardening
- ☐ Bird Watching
- ☐ Astronomy/Stargazing
- ☐ Science Experimenting
- ☐ Collecting Things

Hobby Aids
Some tools are mentioned here briefly. For more complete lists see "Tools" in the Storage section and also in "Outdoor Garden & Maintenance" in the Outdoor Living and Maintenance section. More sewing supplies are given in Storage under "Sewing Kit."

- ☐ Camera Equipment, Film, & Darkroom Equipment
- ☐ Video Camera/Camcorder
- ☐ Movie Camera, Projector & Screen
- ☐ Slide Projector
- ☐ View Master

Art & Crafts Supplies
- ☐ Canvas
- ☐ Easel
- ☐ Tote Board
- ☐ Sketching Pad
- ☐ Special Paper (i.e. Watercolor, Poster Board, Colored, Construction, Transfer, Calligraphy, Art Tissue)
- ☐ Color Wheel
- ☐ Pencils, Assorted
- ☐ Erasers
- ☐ Calligraphy Lettering Set
- ☐ Paints (i.e. Watercolors, Oils, Liquid Tempura, Stencil)
- ☐ Paint Crayons
- ☐ Marking Pens
- ☐ Charcoals

- ☐ Paint Thinner
- ☐ Median
- ☐ X-Acto Knife
- ☐ Mat Cutter
- ☐ Frames & Frame Kits
- ☐ Stapling Tacker & Staples
- ☐ T Square
- ☐ Triangular Square
- ☐ Stencils
- ☐ Sewing Machine & Supplies (i.e. Dress Form, Patterns)
- ☐ Handwork Patterns
- ☐ Knitting Needles & Yarn
- ☐ Crochet Kit
- ☐ Embroidery Kit
- ☐ Needlepoint Kit
- ☐ Weaving Equipment (i.e. Loom or Spinning Wheel) & Supplies
- ☐ Quilting Kit
- ☐ Macrame Kit
- ☐ Art Needlework Mounting Board & Tape
- ☐ Miscellaneous Craft Supplies (i.e. Craft Sticks, Beads, Wires &Sequins; Glue & Stains; Modeling Clay & Spatulas; Ribbons & Lace & Velcro; Decals & Rubber Art Stamps; T-Shirt Art Supplies; Marbelizing Kit; Glue Gun)

☐ Jewelry Making Supplies

Floral Supplies
- ☐ Dried & Artificial Flowers
- ☐ Baskets, Vases, Pots, Wreaths, etc.
- ☐ Planter Moss or Lichen
- ☐ Accessories (i.e. Wire, Tape, Picks, Clay)

☐ Pottery Kit

Music-related Items
- ☐ Musical Instruments
- ☐ Music Stand
- ☐ Sheet Music
- ☐ Instrument Cases and/or Covers
- ☐ Supplies for Cleaning & Repairing Instruments

☐ Shop Tools (i.e. for Metal, Woodworking, Stone, Ceramics, Stained Glass, etc.)

☐ Carpenter's Apron

☐ Lapidary Supplies (i.e. Rock Polisher, Tumbler)

☐ Mechanical Tools (i.e. for Car Repair, etc.)

☐ Hobby Electronics Supplies & Tools (i.e Wire, Batteries, Small Motors, Volt Meter, Soldering Gun)

☐ Model Railroad Supplies

☐ Model Building Kits & Supplies (i.e. Glue, Paint, Brushes)

☐ Gardening Tools

☐ Binoculars

☐ Telescope

☐ Tripod

☐ Magnifying Glass

☐ Science Kits (i.e. Chemistry Set)

☐ Insect Net

- ☐ Miscellaneous Hobby Supplies and Equipment (i.e. Metal Detector)
- ☐ Special Interest & Instruction Books
- ☐ Display Materials for Hobbies & Collections (i.e. Display Cases, Lighting)

Collections

- ☐ Antiques
- ☐ Fine Art
- ☐ Coins
- ☐ Wine
- ☐ Dolls
- ☐ Stuffed Animals
- ☐ Guns
- ☐ Rare Books
- ☐ Model Trains

- ☐ Masks
- ☐ Rocks/Stones
- ☐ Sea Shells
- ☐ Trophies & Medals
- ☐ Stamps
- ☐ Miniatures
- ☐ Memorabilia (i.e. Theater, Sports, Military)
- ☐ Commemorative Pins & Buttons
- ☐ Posters
- ☐ Baseball and/or Other Trading Cards
- ☐ Comic Books
- ☐ Matchbooks
- ☐ Miscellaneous Collectibles

23 The Car

C ar is not meant to be an exclusive term here and easily includes other modes of transportation, such as trucks and vans.

Some of the items listed are things most of us carry inside our vehicles or in their storage spaces (i.e. maps and insurance information). A number of the other things mentioned are included in case of emergency. Extra items are added that are not necessarily carried inside cars but are nevertheless associated with them and/or their care and maintenance.

The Car

In the Car or Trunk

- ☐ Car Insurance Information
- ☐ Car Registration
- ☐ Owner's Manual
- ☐ Emergency Road Service Handbook
- ☐ Auto Association Information & Card
- ☐ Maps
- ☐ Windshield Scraper
- ☐ Spray Bottle of Water
- ☐ A Rag or Two
- ☐ Deodorizer
- ☐ Infant/Child Car Seat
- ☐ Jumper Cables
- ☐ Road Flares
- ☐ Flashlight & Extra Batteries
- ☐ Portable Radio & Extra Batteries

- ☐ A Few Tools
  (i.e. Screwdrivers, Pliers,
  Crescent Wrench)
- ☐ First Aid Kit
- ☐ Water
- ☐ Food Bars
- ☐ Whistle
- ☐ Paper, Pen, or Pencil
- ☐ Dust Masks
- ☐ Blanket
- ☐ Sturdy Shoes
- ☐ Warm Jacket

Also for the Car
- ☐ Tire Chains

- ☐ Luggage Rack
- ☐ Ski Rack
- ☐ Bike Rack
- ☐ Quart of Oil
- ☐ Coolant
- ☐ Transmission Fluid
- ☐ Power Steering Fluid
- ☐ Tire Gauge
- ☐ Whisk Broom
- ☐ Bucket
- ☐ Chamois
- ☐ Car Shampoo
- ☐ Towels
- ☐ Car Wax

24 Safe Places
(Including the Safe Deposit Box)

All of us have important papers and records that require safe keeping. Some of these we may store in a safe deposit box, while others we keep in our homes or workplaces. We may give copies of some of our important information to relatives, trusted friends, attorneys, or bankers in case we lose the originals or for other practical purposes.

Of course, putting your important papers in a safe place is only the beginning. Your estate planning, insurance policies, personal property inventories, and other important documents should be reviewed and updated as your life situation and needs change.

It is also important to keep track of where you put the things you list, noting where the original is, plus any copies.   Each person in your home will need their own, separate list to avoid confusion where there are differences (i.e. birth certificates, retirement papers, driver's license numbers, and so on).

Additionally, we may keep certain valuables like jewelry or coins in a safe or safe deposit box. If you have a safe in your home, it should be fire-proof (rather than fire-resistant) to withstand heat up to 4,000 degrees. The best place for a safe is in the basement, partially submerged in concrete and bolted to the floor.

Safe Places

- [ ] Will (Plus Codicils, if applicable)
- [ ] List of Special Bequests
- [ ] Titles & Deeds, Including Mortgages
- [ ] Lease Agreements
- [ ] Notes & Loan Agreements
- [ ] Lines of Credit
- [ ] Birth Certificate
- [ ] Marriage License
- [ ] Citizenship Papers

Insurance Policies
- [ ] Health
- [ ] Auto
- [ ] Property (Homeowners or Renters)
- [ ] Life
- [ ] Disability
- [ ] Business
- [ ] Title
- [ ] Other (i.e. Professional Liability)
- [ ] Powers of Attorney
- [ ] Durable Power of Attorney for Health Care
- [ ] Trust Agreements & Documents
- [ ] Employment Contracts
- [ ] Partnership Agreements
- [ ] Business Agreements/ Contracts
- [ ] Auto Ownership Certificate
- [ ] Boat Records
- [ ] House Plans/Blueprints
- [ ] Financial Plan

Investment Records
- [ ] Brokerage Account Records
- [ ] Stock Certificates
- [ ] Mutual Fund Records
- [ ] Certificates of Deposit
- [ ] Bonds
- [ ] Limited Partnerships
- [ ] Other Securities
- [ ] Deferred Compensation
- [ ] IRA or Keough Plans
- [ ] Annuity Contracts
- [ ] Stock-option Plan
- [ ] Stock-purchase Plan
- [ ] Profit-sharing Plan
- [ ] Income & Gift Tax Returns
- [ ] Tax Returns
- [ ] Bank Statements & Cancelled Checks
- [ ] Retirement Papers
- [ ] Pension Plans
- [ ] Military Discharge Papers

Public Benefits Records
- [ ] Social Security
- [ ] Worker's Compensation Benefits
- [ ] Public Medical Insurance
- [ ] Job Training Program Services

Court Decrees
- [ ] Divorce/Separation Records
- [ ] Adoption Papers
- [ ] Custody and/or Guardianship Papers
- [ ] Lawsuit Settlements

☐ Passport

Record of Important Numbers
(Plus their Addresses, Phone
Numbers & Cancellation
Instructions, if applicable)

☐   Social Security

☐   Driver's License

☐   Checking Accounts

☐   Savings Accounts

☐   Credit Cards

☐   Safe Combination

Medical Records & Health
History

☐   Major Illnesses, Accidents
& Medical conditions

☐   Prescriptions

☐   Known Allergies

☐   Summary of
Immunizations

☐   Hospitalizations,
Including Surgeries

☐   Family Health Histories

☐   Physicians & Medical
Centers Used

☐   Directive to Physicians

Keepsake Documents

☐   Diplomas

☐   Awards, Certificates of
Merit, Honors

☐   Religious Certificates (i.e
Baptismal, Bar Mitzvah,
etc.)

☐ Professional Licensure,
Certification, etc.

☐ Student Transcripts

☐ Records of Family
Histories/Genealogies

☐   Journals

☐   Manuscripts

☐   Computer Disks

☐   Purchase Agreements &
Records, including Warranties

☐   Before-need Funeral
Instructions

☐   Cemetery Plot Deeds

☐   List of Stored or Loaned
Items

☐   List of Debts or Money Owed
to you

List of Contacts with Names &
Addresses

☐   Relatives & Friends

☐   Professional, Fraternal &
Other Organizations &
Memberships

☐   Business Contacts,
Associates, Prospects

List of Safe or Safe Deposit Items
in Addition to Papers

☐   Jewelry

☐   Coins or Coin
Collections

☐   Cash

Personal Property Inventory

☐   General Written Inventory

☐   Appraisals

☐   List of Valuables (i.e.
Antiques, Family
Heirlooms, Jewelry)

☐   Photo Record (Snapshots
and/or Video) of
Household Inventory &
Other Personal Property

25 Shopping Green

Shopping Green reflects the growing concern of Americans about the environment. Surveys suggest that most of us want to do our part to make the world a better place. We are recycling more, and we are becoming more selective about what we buy. "Shop till you drop," a popular slogan, bumper sticker, and ethic of the 1980s appears to be a rapidly diminishing and outdated mindset for the 90s as we become more aware of the connection between overconsumption and environmental problems.

In June, 1992, delegates from more than 170 nations met in Rio de Janeiro, Brazil, to wrestle with environmental and development issues at the United Nations Earth Summit. But regardless of what treaties, goals, rules, regulations, and laws come from nations and governments, each one of us as individuals has decisions to make about how to respond to environmental concerns. And because we vote with our dollars, we need to learn how we can make our purchases reflect our caring.

This section attempts to provide some suggestions to help you make your home an environmentally friendly place. What is included here will be minimal compared to the vast amout of information available. Not being an expert myself, I will refer you to those who are. For example, much of the information here is gleaned from the books, *The Green Consumer* and *50 Things You can Do To Save The Earth* (see Sources). These and other books and resources outline and explain major environmental problems, providing easy-to-understand technical information as well as serving as guides for what to do and buy.

The bad news is that we have a number of serious environmental problems. *The Green Consumer* lists the following: acid rain, global warming and the greenhouse effect, ozone depletion, air pollution, the destruction of rain forests and decreasing biodiversity, garbage, and water pollution.

The encouraging news is that there is something we can do as individuals about each one of them. By shopping "green," for instance, we can conserve energy, reduce garbage, and buy products that don't pollute the air and water. Some of the early Americans showed tremendous insight in a law that they expressed in the Six Nations Iroquois Confederacy: "In our every deliberation, we must consider the impact of our decisions on the next seven generations."

Shopping Green means choosing products that cause a minimal impact on the environment, either because of the products themselves or because of their packaging or both. The ideal green product doesn't endanger the health of people or animals; it doesn't damage the environment during its manufacture, use, or disposal; it doesn't consume a disproportionate amount of energy while it is being manufactured, used, or disposed of; it doesn't cause unnecessary waste, due either to its excessive packaging or to a short useful life; it doesn't involve the unnecessary use of or cruelty to animals; and it doesn't use materials derived from threatened species or environments.

To buy or not to buy–that is the question to consider here. It requires us to determine what to avoid and how to figure out the alternatives. Following is a list of some of the substances detrimental to the environment. We are told to avoid them because of what they are or contain, because of the way they are manufactured, because of what they may or do cause, or because of further difficulties when disposed of.

Carbon Dioxide
Carcinogenic Chemicals
Chlorides
Chlorine
Chlorofluorocarbons (CFCs)
Corrosive Ingredients &
Poisons
Dioxins
Halons
Hydocarbons
Methane

Nitrogen-based Fertilizer
Nitrous Oxide
Nonbiodegradable Materials
Ozone Smog
Pesticides
Phosphates
Poisonous Metals
Polyethylene
Polystyrene

The first thing we can do is precycle. That means buying less in the first place. It also means making environmentally sound decisions while we shop by noticing the packaging (and avoiding plastic goods, overpackaged items, and what can't be reused, refilled, or recycled), not buying disposable items (like razors, diapers, or Styrofoam cups), and buying in bulk. Bringing our own reusable bags on shopping trips saves on paper and plastic.

Taking into consideration the major environmental problems mentioned that we can do something about, the list of detrimental substances to avoid, and the concept of precycling, we can review a number of items and categories in *The Household Inventory Guide* to help determine what to buy and what not to buy. We won't however, follow the order of the book, section by section, because of the overlap of many of the categories of household items or products mentioned throughout the book.

In the next pages we will examine the following areas to help discover ways to become effective consumers: appliances, lighting, furniture, household cleaners, saving water, household paper products, plastics, cosmetics and personal care products, hazardous waste, and recycling.

Appliances

As of 1990 the federal government established minimum efficiency standards for major home appliances and heating and cooling equipment. The most energy-efficient appliances cost more but save money in the long run as they use up to 50 percent less energy than the most wasteful ones.

The ten biggest home energy users are

Water Heaters	Dishwashers
Clothes Washers	Air Conditioners
Refrigerators/Freezers	Portable Space Heaters
Clothes Dryers	Ranges
Freezers	Lighting

Some of the above appliances are required to disclose their energy efficiency ratings. You will find their EERs or annual energy costs on the attached Energy Guide labels.

For a complete list of appliance energy ratings you can get a booklet for a couple of dollars called "The Most Energy-Efficient Appliances" from the American Council for an Energy-Efficient Economy. Contact

ACEEE
1101 Connecticut Ave. NW, Suite 535
Washington, DC 20036
(202) 429-8873

Lighting

Since the 1800s, we've been mostly using standard light bulbs known as incandescent bulbs. The most durable of these lasts about 1,000 hours. Now we have choices. Compact fluorescents last ten times longer than the incandescents and use about 90 percent less electricity. High-intensity discharge (HID) bulbs increase lamp life up to four times that of a standard bulb but require special fixtures and can become very hot. In 1993, production is scheduled on a limited basis for a light known as an electronic light or "E-Lamp," which will last up to 20,000 hours and use 75 percent less energy.

Not surprisingly, alternative lighting costs more to buy in the beginning, but the newer types save on your energy bill. If you can't find them in your local hardware or lighting supply store, you can find lists of places where they can be ordered in books and magazines about environmental consumerism.

Furniture

Every year millions of acres of tropical rainforests are destroyed, with some of the wood being used to make furniture. Mahogany, teak, ramin, lauan, and meranti are some of the timbers used for this purpose. When you are shopping for furniture, look instead for woods such as ash, beech, birch, cherry, elm, hickory, oak, poplar, and black walnut.

To get more information on rainforests and to find out what else you can do to preserve them besides buying alternatives to tropical hardwoods, contact

> The Rainforest Action Network
> 301 Broadway, Suite A
> San Francisco, CA 94133
> (415) 398-4404

The contents of furniture is also worth considering as many cushions are made from plastic foam containing CFCs or methylene chloride, a probable carcinogenic. Also, if these substances burn, they emit toxic gases.

Household Cleaners

A lot of the products that we have come to depend on to clean our clothes, dishes, ovens, floors, toilets, carpets, and so on contain toxic substances. They can be dangerous to ourselves and harmful to the environment.

There are, however, plenty of nonpolluting alternative cleaning products and methods available. *The Green Consumer* lists a number of nontoxic, biodegradable, and often cruelty-free products as well as the companies that sell them. It also gives recipes for making your own natural cleaners out of the ingredients you probably already have, such as baking soda, vinegar, lemon juice, vegetable oil, borax, and hot water. Instructions are provided for the following natural products:

Air Fresheners	Glass Cleaner
All-purpose Cleaners	Insect Repellants
Carpet Deodorizers	Laundry Products
Dishwashing Liquids	Metal Polishes
Disinfectants	Mold & Mildew Cleaners
Drain Cleaners	Mothballs
Flea & Tick Control	Oven Cleaners
Floor Cleaners	Pesticides
Floor & Furniture Polish	Toilet Cleaners

Other sources of information include two books by Debra Lynn Dadd, *The Nontoxic Home* and *Nontoxic, Natural and Earthwise*. *The Nontoxic Home* gives background information on how to decide which home products are healthy and safe, and *Nontoxic, Natural and Earthwise* rates the toxicity of 1,200 brand-name products. It also provides lists of mail-order sources for safe products and includes do-it-yourself formulas for common household products.

Saving Water

Water-saving devices are usually easy to come by. They are sold at hardware stores, houseware departments of department stores, and sometimes at water companies. There are three products that will save you hundreds of gallons of water in no time at all: toilet dams, low-flow faucet aerators, and low-flow shower heads.

Toilet dams or displacement bags save water every time you flush. Sometimes two dams can be installed in one toilet, but never use a brick because it can disintegrate in the tank. If you are buying a new toilet, consider the newest development, the "ultra low-flush" toilet. Obviously, a leaky toilet wastes water.

You can test for a leak by adding food coloring or a special tablet to the toilet tank.

By installing low-flow faucet aerators on all faucets, you can reduce flow by 50 percent. Low-flow shower heads cut shower flow by 2 to 2 1/2 gallons a minute.

Household Paper Products

Aside from the fact that paper comes from trees, one of our valuable and diminishing resources, many of our paper products contain traces of dioxins, a family of toxic, carcinogenic chemicals formed during the chlorine bleaching process of papermaking.

The presence of dioxins has been found in products such as paper towels, toilet paper, facial tissues, tampons, disposable diapers, milk cartons, and coffee filters. Not only do these chemicals end up in the paper, they have also been discovered downstream from pulp and mills where they have contaminated water for fish and soil for crops. They are also released into the air when paper products are disposed of in a landfill or are incinerated.

Higher grade papers go through fewer bleaching stages and so contain less dioxin. Newsprint is not bleached at all. Recycled papers require either no bleaching or much less bleaching than other papers.

It is easier to find recycled paper products than unbleached paper because of the low demand for the latter in the U.S. Sources for both, however, are listed in *The Green Consumer.* Two companies that offer recycled/unbleached paper towels, toilet paper, napkins, and facial tissue are

C.A.R.E. Products
Ashdun Industries, Inc.
1605 John St.
Fort Lee, NJ 07024
(201)944-2650

Marcel Paper Mills, Inc.
Market St.
Elmwood Park, NJ 0707
(201) 796 4000
(800) 631-8451

Melitta U.S.A., Ashdun Industries, and Natural Brew all make unbleached coffee filters. Reusable filters are made from cotton and last for about a year. These and permanent gold mesh coffee filters are available at kitchen supply, gourmet coffee shops, and department stores.

Besides reusable coffee filters, other things can substitute for paper products, such as cloth napkins for the paper kind and cleaning rags in place of paper towels.

Plastics

Plastics are troublesome for the environment because many of the chemicals used in their production and processing are highly toxic and because they contribute to our solid waste problem. According to *The Green Consumer,* "The single largest use of plastics today is in packaging, constituting a fourth of the 12 billion or so pounds of plastics produced each year in this country." And packaging accounts for almost a third of all trash discarded by the average American.

Common household plastics include bags, wraps, films, jars, jugs, foams, tampons, and disposable diapers.

Polystyrene foam (as in Styorofoam cups, food trays, and some egg cartons, and so on) is completely non-biodegradable and is made by a process using CFC gases which eat ozone molecules.

Tampons with plastic applicator tubes often end up in our rivers, streams, and oceans where they are mistaken for food by fish and birds. Tampax brand tampon applicators, however, are made from biodegradable cardboard.

It is estimated that disposable diapers, made with polyethylene resin, will take between 300 and 500 years to break down. More than 18 billion disposable diapers are dumped each year into America's landfills along with 3 million tons of untreated feces and urine containing over 100 different intestinal viruses.

Cotton diapers, obviously better for the environment, also cost less than the disposables—even, in certain areas, if you order them from a delivery service. You can buy cloth diapers at department stores or from the following companies, which also sell cloth covers and other diapering products:

Bio-Bottoms
P.O. Box 6009
3820 Bodega Ave.
Petaluma, CA 94953

Baby Bunz and Company
P.0. Box 1717
Sebastopol CA 95473

Alternative sandwich-size or freezer-size bags, which are made from plant fiber and are nontoxic and biodegradable, may be ordered from

Seventh Generation
10 Farrell St.
South Burlington, VT 05403
(802) 862-2999
(800) 456-1177

Co-Op America
2100 M St. NW, Suite 310
Washington, DC 20036
(202) 872-5307
(800) 658-5507

Earth Care Paper Co.
100 S. Baldwin
Madison, WI 53703
(608) 256-5522

Ecco Bella
125 Pompton Plains
Crossroads
Wayne, NJ 07470
(201) 890-7077

You can get biodegradable trash bags from

Webster Industries
58 Pulaski St.
P.O. Box 3119
Peabody, MA 01960
(508) 532-2000

Yard wastes can be collected in the Ecolobag from

Dano Enterprises, Inc.
75 Commercial St.
Plainview, NY 11803
(516) 349-7300

Cosmetics and Personal Care Products

Millions of laboratory animals (mice, rats, dogs, rabbits, monkeys, and so on) die or are disfigured each year when they are used in testing for such commercial household products as shampoo, shaving cream, mouthwash, suntan oil, hand lotion, face cream, mascara, and perfume.

The Green Consumer lists companies that do not test on animals and those that do. These lists were compiled by People for the Ethical Treatment of Animals (PETA) in Washington, DC. Also mentioned are mail-order companies that feature cruelty-free and environmentally friendly companies.

Even some of the large, well-known manufacturers and retail stores are coming out with environmentally friendly product lines in everything from cosmetics, body and bath care, bedding, clothes, and accessories. Estee Lauder, for example, launched a new company called Origens in 1990 that makes botanicals-based natural skin care products using recyclable and non-animal tested or derived materials.

Levi Strauss & Co. and Esprit de Corp are beginning to produce environmentally sensitive apparel–clothing made out of organic and/or undyed, unbleached materials. Stores like Macy's and I. Magnin are paying attention to a growing consumer base interested in natural products.

When shopping for apparel, it's best to choose clothes that don't have to be dry cleaned, because dry cleaners use solvents that emit fumes that greatly contribute to urban smog.

Hazardous Waste

Hazardous waste can have damaging effects on our soil, air, and water, not to mention the human population and all other living things. We can try to avoid it as much as possible in our homes, as well as learn to store it properly and recycle what we can. *The Green Consumer* addresses all these issues, plus gives alternative solutions and products for many of them.

Following is a list of some of the things commonly found in our households which are considered to be hazardous waste:

Abrasive Cleaners or Powders
Ammonia-based Cleaners
Bleach Cleaners
Disinfectants
Drain Cleaners
Floor & Furniture Polish
Household Batteries
Mothballs
Oven Cleaners
Photographic Chemicals
Pool Chemicals
Rug & Upholstery Cleaners
Toilet Cleaners
Paints
Furniture Strippers
Stains & Finishes
Thinners & Turpentine
Aerosol Spray Cans
Pesticides
    Insecticides
    Soil Fumigants
    Pet Sprays
    Snail & Slug Poisons
    Rat, Mouse & Gopher Poisons
Car Batteries
Antifreeze & Coolants
Brake Fluids
Used Motor Oils
Gasoline

Many commercial paint products are manufactured from nonrenewable sources such as crude oil, but a growing number of paints are made from natural materials through a safer process. Three companies that make natural paint products are

AFM Enterprise
1140 Stacy Ct.
Riverside, CA 930507
(714) 781-6860

Auro Organic Paints
P.O. Box 181
Suisun City, CA 94585
(707) 427-2325

Livos Plant Chemistry
2641 Cerrillos Rd.
Santa Fe, NM 87501
(505) 988-9111

To get a free brochure on the best way to dispose of paint, contact

National Paint & Coating Association
1500 Rhode Island Ave. NW
Washington, DC 20005

An alternative to the dry-cell batteries we use for our flashlights, radios, cameras, and so on is to get the rechargable kind and a recharger. Most of these batteries can be recharged up to 1,000 times. Regular household batteries contain toxic metals that can leak and corrode. They can be recycled, however. If you don't know of a site in your area that accepts them, one company assists local community groups in setting up recycling programs. For more information contact

Mercury Refining Company
790 Watervilet Shaker Rd.
Latham, NY 12110
(518) 785-1703
(800) 833-3505

You can find out more about hazardous waste in *Hazardous Waste from Homes* from Enterprise for Education, 1320 A 3rd St., Suite 202, Santa Monica, CA 90401 or call Laidlaw Environmental Services at (800) 845-1019. Laidlaw also can help you start a hazardous waste collection day in your area.

If you have questions regarding pesticides, you can call the EPA's 24-hour-a-day hotline at (800) 858-7378.

Recycling

Almost all household items can be reused or recycled. The following list is compiled from ads and articles in one phone book's yellow pages and a local newpaper:

Paper
- Newspaper
- Magazines
- Corrugated Cardboard
- White Paper
- Colored Paper
- Computer Paper
- Old Office Files & Records
- Milk & juice Cartons

Glass
- Bottles
- Jars

Plastic
- Beverage Bottles
- Milk Jugs
- Detergent Bottles
- Aspirin Bottles
- Cooking Oil Bottles
- Microwave Food Trays
- Bags & Wrap
- Clean Polystyrene Pellets

Metal
- Aluminum Cans & Scrap
- Tin Cans
- Scrap Metals
- Brass
- Copper
- Stainless Steel
- Steel
- Precious Metals
- Electronic Scrap
- Insulated Copper Wire
- Bottle Caps

Car Parts
- Motor Oil
- Antifreeze & Coolant
- Batteries
- Tires
- Auto Body Parts

Building & Salvage Materials
- Wood
- Concrete & Asphalt
- Bricks
- Cabinets
- Doors
- Windows
- Tiles
- Light Fixtures
- Toilets
- Nails
- Plumbing

Appliances
Washers
Dryers
Stoves
Refrigerators
Air Conditioning Units
TVs
VCRs
Stereos
Computers
Office Equipment
File Cabinets
Typewriters
Printers
Office Machines
Calculators

Miscellaneous
Yard Wastes (Grass,
Prunings,etc.)
Material for Children's
Art Projects
Household Goods
(Kitchenware & Tools)
Box Springs
Paint
Floppy Disks
Cork
Furniture
Clothes
Scientific Instruments

To locate a nearby recycling program, call the Environmental Defense Fund's hotline at (800) 225-5333. You can also request brochures on home and office recycling and a resource list of publications and organizations.

An excellent book on recyling or disposing of most household items is *Complete Trash—The best way to get rid of practically everything around the house* by Norm Crampton (Little, Brown & Co.).

Sources for Further Sleuthing & Shopping

Books
• *50 Simple Things You Can Do To Save The Earth*
  by The Earth Works Group, Earthworks Press, Berkeley, CA.
  Also by Earth Works Press
    • *The Next Step: 50 More Things You Can Do To Save The Earth*

- *50 Simple Things Businesses Can Do To Save The Earth*
- *50 Simple Things Kids Can Do To Recycle*
- *The Recycler's Handbook*

- *The Green Consumer* by John Elkington, Julia Hailes, and Joel Makower, Penguin Books.

- *Shopping For A Better World–A Quick and Easy Guide to Socially Responsible Shopping* by Ben Corson, Alice Tepper Marlin, Jonathan Schorsch, Anitra Swaminathan, and Rosalyn Will, Council on Economic Priorities and Ballantine Books.

Also look for local resources. For instance, the following book is a good one in my area:
- *Bay Area Green Pages– The Local Handbook for Planet Maintenance* by Green Media Group, Eric Ingesoll Publisher, P.O. Box 11314, Berkeley, CA 94701, (510) 534-3470.

Phone Tips
On Consumer Information
The Pennsylvania Resources Council (PRC) is a nonprofit group dedicated to educating consumers on environmentally sound shopping habits. If you have questions, call them at (800) 468-6772 .
On Energy Conservation
The Conservation and Renewable Energy Inquiry & Referral Service (CAREIRS) will answer your general questions or send you a brochure on insulation, caulking, etc. They can also offer you a free community recycling packet. Their number is (800) 523-2929.
If you have technical questions, engineers will research your problems at the National Appropriate Technology Assistance Service (NATAS), a Department of Energy hotline. Call (800) 428-2525. In Montana call (800) 428-1718.

26 Moving On

M oving is a bit like preparing a meal—
timing is critical to get everything to
come out right. And the more you have on
your plate, the more coordinating you have
to do. This section will be most helpful to
those moving from one home to another, but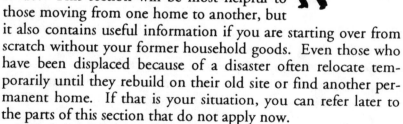
it also contains useful information if you are starting over from
scratch without your former household goods. Even those who
have been displaced because of a disaster often relocate temporarily until they rebuild on their old site or find another permanent home. If that is your situation, you can refer later to
the parts of this section that do not apply now.

Let's assume for our purposes here that the legal and financial
aspects of your move have have been settled. Escrow has closed
or your tenant's agreement signed. Dates have been set for
moving out of your old home and into your new place. We will
deal here with the planning, logistics, and details of the move.

A major consideration in the beginning is how you will move.
This will depend on a number of factors including how far you
are moving, how much you have to move, and who is paying for
your move. You may be able to load your belongings in your
vehicle and do it yourself; you may plan to rely on family or
friends and a rented trailer or truck; perhaps you are being re-
located by an organization that is willing to do much of the

work for you and pay for it, too; or you may contract with a professional moving company.

If you choose the latter, be sure to get personal references from your realtor, friends, or the moving companies themselves. Because all carriers are not created equal, a friend of mine in the moving business suggests reading an August, 1990 article in *Consumer Reports* called "Surviving Your Next Move" which reviews major van lines.

Authorized carriers will give you a written estimate or "probable cost of services." You should also get information regarding rules, regulations, and rate requirements if you are moving or storing your things within the same state. In California the regulatory agency is called the Public Utilities Commission, which requires all carriers to distribute a booklet to persons planning to move their household goods between points in California. Every state has such an agency, but they go by different names (i.e. Public Service Commission).

The moving company you select will coordinate and confirm dates and times with you and will give you a complete list of their services and products. Then you can decide who does the packing and unpacking, for instance, or whether you want to use their packing cartons.

In addition to the actual period of moving, you will have other dates to consider and coordinate. The following companies need to be contacted to disconnect and connect utilities and to discontinue and begin services:

Telephone
    For local & long distance services
    To install phone jacks, if needed
Heating (i.e. Gas, Electric, Propane, Fuel Oil, Coal)
Water
Garbage
Cable TV (If you are a renter, you may need a letter from your landlord giving the cable company permission to drill holes.)

Other companies and organizations also need to be notified that you are moving. When you contact the insurance company that issues your homeowners or renters policy, they may offer you a "rider" to insure your household goods while they are in transit. Know whether your moving company, if you have one, accepts liability for the mechanical or electrical derangement of such items as pianos, phonographs, clocks, televisions, refrigerators, computers, and so on. If you plan to rent space for storage, ask your insurance agent about coverage.

If you have daily or weekly newspaper delivery, be sure to cancel before moving on, and order whatever paper(s) you want to be delivered to your new address.

Banks and other financial institutions need to be apprised of your move, and you will need to order checks in your new location. You may want to wait until you know your phone number, however, before ordering your checks. If you are changing bank companies, you will need to close out old accounts and open new ones. Also, if your are moving out of the area and have a safe deposit box, remember to transfer the contents and move them into a new box.

If your move is outside your present neighborhood, you may need to arrange to have medical, dental, financial, and school records transferred to your new location. Also, to re-register to vote, contact the County Clerk's office.

Whenever you move, you must cross out your address on the front of your driver's license and write your new address on the back. If you move to another state, you will need to re-apply for a new license altogether and also re-register all vehicles.

The U.S. Post Office will provide you with two types of cards to complete. One goes directly to your local post office so that they have the information they need to forward your mail to your new address. The other is a change of address request form which is actually a post card, so you will need an adequate supply of stamps.

Following is a list of correspondents, publishers, and businesses for you to use as a basis for your change of address cards. It's a good idea to keep a list of names and addresses in a convenient location in order to keep track of those you've sent, because you may need to add to your list, and sometimes you have to send a second card.

Magazines & Other Subscriptions
Catalogs
Internal Revenue Service
State Franchise Board
Department of Motor Vehicles
Credit Card Companies or Stores whose cards you hold
Banks and Savings & Loan Companies
Brokerage and/or Investment Firms
Insurance Companies
Organizations
    Employer
    Business & Professional
    Charitable
    Schools (Present and/or Former)
    Church, Synagogue, etc.
    Political Party
    Public and/or Special Interest Groups
    Fraternal
    Social
    Other Membership Groups

If you no longer wish to receive mail from certain businesses or organizations, use the change of address forms to indicate that. Simply leaving the new address section blank should let recipients know that you want to be deleted from their mailing list.

To reduce "junk mail," write to the Direct Mail/Marketing Association at 6 East 43rd St., New York, NY 10017 and ask to be eliminated from mailing lists.

Most magazines, newsletters, catalogs, journals and the like have labels that can be removed and taped over the old address section of the change of address request form. Publishers and others who provide the labels prefer that you use them because the labels usually contain valuable coded information that helps them process changes.

You can also use the postal change of address post cards to let family, friends, and associates know where you are moving, or you may want to let them know in a more personal way. For example, stationery and other stores carry notes that announce your change of address. You may also want to order new business cards, address labels and/or rubber stamps, letterhead or personal stationery that give your new address.

Moving seems to be a time for making all kinds of lists. One to consider is a list of your expenditures. I have always found moving to be costly–whether I used a professional moving company or not. I think that's because when we change locations, we think of making other changes as well. Things that work well or suffice in our present home no longer fit or seem appropriate in our new place. The old refrigerator turns out to be the wrong size, and the sofa begins to look too shabby to take along. So, we repair, refinish, refurbish, and shop.

I am always amazed when I tally up my moving-related expenses. And it's not just because of major purchases, which I may or may not make. There are a seemingly endless number of nickel-dime expenses. Just changing your phone number and establishing other utilities and services can cost plenty.

Hardware stores are among our beneficiaries as we move into our new homes and notice all the things that need doing or fixing or upgrading and, thus, require our spending–additional door keys, more picture hooks, a new door mat, heavier window shades, a full-length mirror, shelf-lining paper, a longer phone cord, water-saving devices, door safety latches, insulation materials, closet hooks, paint, and on and on. You may want to keep a running list of everything you can think of that you want to replace, as well as items that reflect your new needs–the little picayune things, along with any major anticipated purchases.

What we buy for our new homes, while taking finances into account, will partly depend on the size of rooms and spaces in the new place. That requires taking lots of measurements, not only of the new home but also of the appliances, furniture, and furnishings that we expect to take with us. We want to make sure they fit, and we need to think about where to put them.

Moving requires us to make lots of decisions, some of them oriented toward future purchases. Others are about what we decide not to take with us and are made during the process of sorting.

If you are one of those people who never throws anything away, chances are that moving will force the issue. As you decide what to take with you and what to leave behind, also consider how to get rid of what you no longer want. You have a number of options. You can sell, donate or otherwise give away, recycle, or dump.

If you have a lot of things that you would like to sell, you might consider having a garage or sidewalk sale. Local newspapers have special sections that advertise these sales, and some even offer garage sale kits to help you get organized. If you have just a few items worth selling, you can list them in the appropriate section or sections in the classifieds, along with your phone number. Used book stores may be interested in buying the books you are finished with. You may be able to sell old or unwanted major appliances to individuals or shops that recondition and resell them.

Some of the things you no longer need or want may have value to those who don't have them. There are many charitable organizations that will gladly pick up your discards and, later, resell them. Call the various thrift shops in your area to find out what they will accept. Some of them have become quite choosy. At the same time, check their pick-up schedules for your neighborhood. Appointments sometimes need to be made weeks in advance. If you don't have enough items to warrant a pick-up, you can drop them off yourself at local drop-off centers or at the thrift shops.

Before you throw anything away, determine if, how, and where your leftovers can be recycled. Glass, aluminum, and newspapers are usually easy to get rid of. Others things are less convenient to dispose of, but many of your discards can be recycled, including old paint cans and other materials considered to be hazardous waste. For more information see the subsection "Recycling" in **Shopping Green** (pages 91-92).

If you still have a lot of to get rid of, you can parcel out the extra trash over a period of time in your weekly garbage pick-ups. Or you can take them to a local landfill. It may also be possible to rent a dumpster from your garbage collection company.

There are at least two instances I can think of when we tend to get mad at ourselves for having put off what we should have done long ago–selling our cars and moving. At these times we feel obliged to get our cars and our homes in the best possible condition, which means that we don't get to enjoy the fruit of our labor or our expenditures.

Moving is a time of doing projects–repairing, repainting, remodeling, restocking, and cleaning. Depending on your circumstances, these projects may be expected on either or both ends of the move. You need to decide what needs doing in the old home and in the new one, and who will do the various projects.

In addition to the actual structural parts of these homes that may need attention (i.e. floors, walls, windows, showers, etc.) notice any furniture or appliances that need work. If you are moving locally and plan to hire an expert to help you with a project, try to coordinate the timing so that whatever is being worked on can be delivered to your new residence. Do the same for any purchases of large items so that you don't have to move them. For instance, the last time I moved, I had a table refinished, and I bought a sofa. I arranged for both to be delivered to my new home as soon as I moved in.

As you make a list of your cleaning projects, notice what can be done comfortably ahead of the move and what must be done at the last minute or after you move. Decide whether or not you will do it all yourself, or whether you will need help. If you hire a cleaning person or service, make sure you know who is responsible for providing the cleaning equipment and supplies.

Following is a list of things or areas that may require cleaning:

Windows (Inside & Outside)

Window Coverings (Drapes, Curtains, Blinds, Shutters, etc.)

Floors
Carpets & Rugs
Appliances (Stove, Refrigerator, etc.)
Fireplace
Bath and/or Shower Areas
Sinks & Countertops
Cupboards (Inside & Surfaces)
Closets
Ceilings (Dust for spider webs.)
Walls (Fill in holes from pictures & other wall hangings.)
Garage, Basement, or Other Storage Areas
Yard, Deck, Porch, Patio, or Other Outdoor Areas

Like cleaning projects, which can be spread out over a period of time or done all at once, packing can take days or weeks. If done by a moving company, it can be finished in a matter of hours.

If you plan to do the packing yourself, you will need to get your own containers and other packing materials. Many retail stores are happy to have you take their used boxes off their hands, but you will have to find out what are the best times to pick them up.

Whether or not you plan to use a professional carrier for your move, you can buy packing boxes and unprinted sheets of newsprint from moving companies. Some truck and trailer rental companies also sell packing materials. Cartons come in various sizes, and some serve very specialized purposes. For example, you can get cartons for mattresses, mirrors or paintings, lamps, and hanging clothes. Some moving companies sell used boxes at reduced prices. Find out if you can resell the cartons you use to a carrier or, at least, return them for recycling. The moving company can also sell you packing tape, or you can buy it a hardware store.

If you need packing material other than unprinted newsprint, consider using "Eco-Foam" instead of polystyrene pellets or bubble wrap. Although they serve the same purpose, Eco-Foam is produced from cornstarch. If you don't want to save it for later use, throw it on your lawn and turn the garden hose on it, or put it in your kitchen sink and run water over it. It will decompose easily and safely. To find out who distributes Eco-Foam in your area contact

American Excelsior Company
P.O. Box 5624
Arlington, TX 76005
(817) 640-2161

If you are moving a short distance and will be making a number of small trips, you can use shopping and garbage bags and suitcases for some of your less bulky things.

Not to belabor the obvious, but if you have a large amount of things to pack, you will have a lot of unpacking to do on the other end. To avoid the frustration of wading through stacks and stacks of boxes, there are a couple of things you can do. You can label, and you can prioritize.

Decide in advance, if possible, what room you want each box to be placed in at the new home, and label it accordingly. You can also list some of the contents like Extra Bedding, Records & Tapes, Pots & Pans, and Work-related Books & Papers so that you have a sense of where to put them away in a particular room or space.

Unless you have very few boxes to move, it will probably take you a long time to unpack and settle in. It's a good idea to do some sorting and prioritizing before you move so you know what to unpack right away. Think in terms of what you will need first or most for the first day or two, and label your boxes, Top Priority, along with an overview of the contents. For instance, you will need certain clothes, personal items, bedding, towels, cooking items, and dishware almost as soon as you begin to unpack. If you are unsure about how to prioritize, **The Short List** (pages 6-12) will guide you through a number of categories to help you make your selections.

When labeling your cartons, also mark Fragile on breakable or valuable items. Some of your things, boxed or not, may require special care. For example, when moving a personal computer, park the hard disk using the program often included on the diagnostic diskette. Put an old or blank disk in the floppy disk drive, and close the drive.

When moving a stereo, fasten down the tone arm, tighten turntable screws, and secure the dustcover. For a compact disc player, check instructions to secure the lazer. Heat can warp discs, so don't move them in a vehicle that may get hot.

To protect fine furniture and antiques against scratches, apply a heavy coat of wax.

Some moving companies suggest that you not ship money, jewelry, important papers, or other valuable personal items, so pack those separately and carry them with you. Also, don't pack matches, flammables, or anything else that may be considered dangerous. The driver of your moving company, if you have one, may make an inventory of all articles shipped on distance moves, but it's a good idea for you to have your own inventory anyway.

If you are planning to move without benefit of professionals, you will probably need helpers–on both ends. Figure out ahead of time what kind of assistance you will need, and get your help and helpers lined up. Do you need to borrow any equipment for the move (i.e. handtruck or dolly, special tools, etc.)? Do you need help packing, unpacking, lifting, disassembling or re-assembling (i.e. beds, stereo, book or display shelving, and so on)? Do you need child care before, during, or after the move or help with your pets? Do you need a warm body to wait in your new home when you can't be there in order for utilities or services to be connected or started (new phone jacks, cable TV, etc.)? Do you need someone to help you center large area rugs or hang drapes? Do you need help connecting or installing your appliances (i.e. washer, dryer, microwave, answering machine, and so on)? Do you need an extra pair of hands and eyes to help you hang pictures?

If you plan to use relatives or friends as unpaid helpers, be sure that you provide them with plenty of food and drink while they are working, and decide whether a note or gift would be appropriate to thank them.

Moving On has covered some distinct aspects of moving such as changing your address, sorting, packing, and so on. There are others, though, that defy categorizing and include a few miscellaneous details.

For example, before you leave your old home, make sure you have removed your Hide-A-Key if you have one. Return anything borrowed, and retrieve anything lent. Disconnect any appliances that should be disconnected, and turn off heating and/or cooling thermostats. Your refrigerator and/or freezer will probably need to be completely emptied at the last minute and your cold food packed or disposed of.

If you are moving from one area to another, be sure that you have the maps you need and a new address book. No matter where you move, keep a utility knife handy for opening boxes all the way up so that you can flatten them when they are empty. Make sure that you have easy access to a few things that you may need right away like drinking glasses, soap, hand towels, toilet paper, and light bulbs. And remember that Murphy's Law is almost always in effect during periods of change. Things will go wrong, but they will go right, too.

27 Afterward About A Forethought
(On Disaster Preparedness)

A number of years ago I attended a workshop during which participants were given an exercise that seems worth repeating here. We were asked to sit down for ten minutes, paper and pen in hand, and make a list of what we would take from our homes if we had to evacuate in a hurry.

The point of the exercise was to help us take a look at our values. What we decided to take from our homes reflected what we considered to be most important to us. Days, even weeks, later I was still coming up with things that I'd forgotten to write down during the short exercise.

Ten minutes isn't much time to think about our most prized possessions and those things that become important to us if we no longer have them anymore. And during an actual emergency, most people don't have the luxury of thinking clearly. Instead, they are asked to act, and to act fast.

Accidents happen. If we can't prevent them, we can at least prepare for them. Two sections in *The Household Inventory Guide* deal with preparedness–**Emergency Supplies** and **Safe Places**. This final section is here as a reminder to plan ahead for what you hope will never happen. You can do this by making and maintaining inventories of your household goods and by noting those items that you would want to take with you in case of emergency.

Anyone having survived a loss of home by disaster knows the importance of keeping accurate inventories for insurance and tax purposes. It is essential, for instance, to have a written inventory of what's in your household, along with descriptions and prices when appropriate. A copy of your inventory should be kept in a safe deposit box or in some location other than your home.

Having a pictorial inventory is also important. Take snap shots of anything of value, such as fine art, antiques, furniture, jewelry, and so on. Note any identification marks like numbers, letters, or signatures on such valuable items as Wedgewood pieces, cut glass, figurines, and so on. These markings should also be noted in any appraisals or certificates of value that you have. Again, one set of prints should be kept off the premises.

A video record is the newest type of inventory and can easily capture the important details of your home (noting special architectural features or custom work), as well as the contents, as it pans each room. You can do this yourself, or you can hire a professional to do it for you. A friend of mine who does this for a living has her clients give their verbal description on film, which can include interesting anecdotes about anything of significance. She suggests to clients that they keep a copy of their video in a safe deposit box or give it to a close relative or friend, but not one in the immediate neighborhood. The yellow pages in my phone book list these services under Video Production Services, although you may also find them under Photographers in other directories.

Whether you review your inventories for ideas or walk through your home room by room noticing those things that mean a lot to you, take time to make a list of what you would want to take with you in case you had to evacuate on short notice. These may include expensive items like jewelry, antiques, and fine art, but also think about those things that have sentimental value such as old letters, genealogies, or a child's first painting. Items of a practical nature like insurance and tax information, property records and other important papers and documents listed in **Safe Places** (pages 76-78) should also be considered along with your collection of emergency supplies.

After you make your basic list, prioritize. Decide what you would grab first, next, and so on. Note the location of each item on your list, and be specific. For instance, photograph albums and family records are at the top of my list, but they are not all in one place. Also, some of them are in plain sight and easy to get to, while others are in a stack of boxes in a closet.

If there are other family members in your home, be sure to share ideas so that everyone has a say in what's important, and everyone knows where to find priority items. Keep your list handy enough for family members to access it easily but not in a place conspicuous enough for an outsider to stumble across it inadvertently.

Also consider how you would gather your priority items together in a hurry in an actual emergency, assuming you have some time available to you. Sadly, survivors of the Oakland-Berkeley firestorm learned after the fact that the best thing to do in such a crisis situation is to think like a burglar. For example, have garbage bags handy, and use the layers of your bedding (excluding a cumbersome bedspread or comforter) to bundle things up and haul them away quickly.

In addition to being a values-related exercise, making an emergency evacuation list and plan is also akin to taking out an insurance policy. We do this to protect ourselves against loss, even as we hope no harm will come to us.

End Note

If you would like to make any additions, corrections, or comments for future editions, please write to Carol Phillips at

IPP Press
P.O. Box 8335
Emeryville, CA 94662-0335

The Household Inventory Guide can be ordered from IPP Press by sending a check or money order for $9.95, plus sales tax (California residents only), plus $1.50 shipping. Quantity discounts are also available.

NOTES

NOTES

NOTES